turn away wrath

MEDITATIONS TO CONTROL ANGER & BITTERNESS

RAND HUMMEL

journey**forth**®

Greenville, South Carolina

Library of Congress Cataloging-in Publication Data

Hummel, Rand, 1956-

Turn away wrath : meditations to control anger and bitterness / Rand Hummel.

p. cm.

Summary: "This is a book of Bible vers. . . . . overcome anger and bitterness"—Provided by publisher.

ISBN-13: 978-1-59166-734-6 (pbk. : alk. paper)

1. Anger—Religious aspects—Christianity—Meditations. 2. Anger—Biblical teaching. 3. Forgiveness of sin—Meditations. 4. Forgiveness of sin—Biblical teaching. 5. Bible—Quotations. I. Title.

BV4627.A5H86 2007

241'.3—dc22

2006036723

Cover Photo Credits: Veer, PhotoDisc, iStockphoto.com.

Turn Away Wrath: Meditations to Control Anger and Bitterness

Design by Craig Oesterling

Composition by Craig Oesterling and Michael Boone

© 2007 by BJU Press

Greenville, South Carolina 29614

JourneyForth Books is a division of BJU Press

Printed in the United States of America

ISBN 978-1-59166-734-6

15 14 13 12 11 10 9 8 7 6 5 4

Table of Contents

Introduction

Dear Reader,

Do you struggle with anger? Would those who know you best describe you as a bitter person? The sins of anger and bitterness have crept into many hearts and most homes. With the high-stress lifestyles and self-centered thinking of most people, uncontrolled anger has grown to become a worldwide crisis.

I grew up an angry kid. Coming from a broken home filled with anger, rage, and bitterness, I learned to handle life the same way. I got in fights through high school and college, blew up at my wife, and was miserable to live with. God used Ephesians 4:26, "Let not the sun go down upon your wrath," to smite my heart. God changed my heart through meditation on His Word.

By God's grace, I can remember losing my temper only three times in the past twenty-five years. Only God could do that.

The simple meditations found in this book are designed to get us to meditate on the very words of God in such a way that the deceitfulness and wickedness of sin are clearly exposed and that hope for victory over out-of-control anger is realized. How can men and women today change the way they handle their anger? By taking heed, guarding their hearts and minds with the very words of God. Please do not get in a hurry. Take your time, even if it means taking three years to get through this book. Think. Meditate. Spend time with each word and word meaning until the truth of what God is saying becomes a part of your life.

Remember, there is no excuse to sin. "There hath no temptation taken you but such as is common to man: but God is faithful, who will not suffer you to be tempted above that ye are able; but will with the temptation also make a way to escape, that ye may be able to bear it" (1 Cor. 10:13). Meditating on the truths of God's Word discussed in this book can be your way of escape.

Don't fall,
Rand Hummel

Meditation

Let's think about it.

Meditation is essential for anyone and everyone who desires to handle anger God's way. Much of this information was covered in *Lest You Fall,* the first book in this series. The same principles of meditation apply whether you are wrestling with impurity, anger, bitterness, or any other life-dominating sin.

The word translated "meditation" throughout Scripture is also translated "imagine" (Ps. 2:1; 38:12), "studieth" (Prov. 15:28; 24:2), "utter, mutter, talk, or speak" (Job 27:4; Ps. 37:30; 71:24; Prov. 8:7); and "mourn" (Isa. 16:7; 38:14; 59:11). It is usually defined as "murmuring," or speaking to oneself. How often do we as believers devote a full morning to studying, imagining, talking through, or speaking to ourselves (meditating) about one specific characteristic of God taught in His Word?

Meditation is a form of creative thinking. Through word studies, comparisons with other passages, and a good study Bible we can understand what God is saying and how to apply it in a life-changing way. For instance, if we set aside an entire hour to "think about" or meditate on how much God loves righteousness and hates evil, our thinking will be affected in such a way that we will personally begin loving good and hating evil more.

Meditation is essential for a full understanding of God's Word. Most of us have developed lazy habits in reading, grammar, syntax, and word study. We often glance over a word we think we know rather than gaze into its true intent and purpose. When Paul uses the phrase "for this cause" (Rom. 1:26; Eph. 5:31; 2 Thess. 2:11, and so forth) it is so easy to keep reading rather than to stop and think, "What cause?" "What is this driving force in Paul's life?" "What was his essential reason for living?" "What is my ultimate reason, purpose, or cause for living?" "Have I attached myself to a cause bigger than myself, my wants, my time, and my life?" Now, Paul's simple phrase "for this cause" takes on a new relevance, and my heart is convicted because I have been living for my own "causes" and not God's!

Meditation is essential for all who seek victory over anger, wrath, and bitterness. Failure in explosive anger, selfish wrath, or cancerous bitterness comes from a lack of knowledge, a misunderstanding of Bible principles, or a misapplication of scriptural truths. We may have read many of the passages that deal with the sins of anger but may not have thought about them in a way that impacts our hearts. How should Proverbs 5:22 influence us as we face an irritating, provoking situation (or person) and are a breath away from exploding in anger? The purpose of this book is to encourage those who desire to free themselves from the bondage of selfish anger to meditate on the very words God wants us to hear that deal with selfish temptations. What God has already given us in His written Word are the very words He would speak to us if we were in a one-on-one counseling situation with Him. As you will see, the over 130 passages dealing with anger, wrath, and bitterness will be dealt with in a meditative way. At the end of this book, you can take what you have learned and begin meditating on other passages of Scripture in the same way.

We can live kind, gentle, forgiving lives free from bondage to the sins of anger and wrath as we begin thinking like God thinks. That takes time! That takes energy! That takes meditation! Now, let's think about it.

"Meditate upon these things; give thyself wholly to them; that thy profiting may appear to all" *(1 Tim. 4:15)*.

Meditation should delight us!

"I will meditate in thy precepts, and have respect unto thy ways. I will delight myself in thy statutes: I will not forget thy word" *(Ps. 119:15–16)*.

"Blessed is the man that walketh not in the counsel of the ungodly, nor standeth in the way of sinners, nor sitteth in the seat of the scornful. But his delight is in the law of the Lord; and in his law doth he meditate day and night" *(Ps. 1:1–2)*.

"My meditation of him shall be sweet: I will be glad in the Lord" *(Ps. 104:34).*

Meditation should consume us!

"Let the words of my mouth, and the meditation of my heart, be acceptable in thy sight, O Lord, my strength, and my redeemer" *(Ps. 19:14).*

"O how love I thy law! It is my meditation all the day" *(Ps. 119:97).*

"Mine eyes prevent the night watches, that I might meditate in thy word" *(Ps. 119:148).*

Meditation should control us!

"This book of the law shall not depart out of thy mouth; but thou shalt meditate therein day and night, that thou mayest observe to do according to all that is written therein: for then thou shalt make thy way prosperous, and then thou shalt have good success" *(Josh. 1:8).*

The Mechanics of Meditation

"How do you do this?"

In some areas of life, there is danger in being a "do-it-yourselfer." I know enough about working on cars to get a job started but often not enough to finish it. Some "do-it-yourself" plumbers, with the goal of simply replacing a faucet, can turn their bathroom into a water park complete with fountains and pools. There are other times when it is essential to be a "do-it-yourselfer." Meditation is one of those times. It is something that we must learn to do ourselves. We can read books, listen to messages, and allow others to meditate for us, or we can study, labor, and master the art of meditation for ourselves. This is definitely a do-it-yourself discipline of the Christian life.

Anyone can meditate. Everyone should meditate. Most don't even try. If you were not interested in controlling your anger and learning to meditate on what God has to say about uncontrolled wrath, you probably would not even be reading this book. What you need is a meditation toolbox that is filled with the proper meditation tools. I would encourage you to get one tool at a time and practice using it until you have mastered it. Don't fall into the trap of filling up your toolbox with specialty tools that you never use.

Tool 1: Your Bible

Read . . . read . . . READ! Read the passage you are studying over and over again. I sometimes type the book or passage out to myself in letter form without any verse or chapter markings. I start with the letter addressed to myself.

> *Dear Rand,*
>
> *Type the passage and then end the letter with—*
>
> > *Your friend,*
> >
> > *Paul, Peter, John, or whoever*

Tool 2: A study Bible

Study Bibles are a tremendous help in understanding the intent and purpose of any given passage. Sometimes a simple clarification of the audience, customs, geographical considerations, or unusual word usages can help you to understand what God was saying to those people at that time. Bible scholars have given their lives to help those who may not have the time or the training to fully understand why God wrote what He wrote in His Word.

Tool 3: Word-study helps

There are many words in our English Bible whose meanings have changed over the years and have almost become obsolete in conversation today. Words such as *concupiscence, superfluity, wantonness, lasciviousness, lucre, guile,* and *quickened* are not found in most of the letters or e-mails we read on a daily basis. Word-study helps such as *Strong's Concordance, Vine's Expository Dictionary, Robertson's New Testament Word Pictures, Vincent's New Testament Word Studies, Theological Wordbook of the Old Testament,* and Greek and Hebrew lexicons open up the meanings to words we commonly glance over as we read. Words are powerful. Because we often do not know the true meanings of certain words, we miss their intent and cannot personally apply the passage as we should.

Tool 4: Bible dictionaries and encyclopedias

Most of us have not grown up in the Holy Land, lived in Egypt, or sailed the Mediterranean. I personally have never fished with a net, hunted with a bow, or plowed with an ox. A good Bible dictionary or encyclopedia can help you feel the heat of the desert and understand the difficulty of sailing through a stormy sea. I would suggest the *International Standard Bible Encyclopedia (ISBE), Zondervan Pictorial Bible Dictionary, Nelson's New Illustrated Bible Dictionary*, or *Unger's Bible Dictionary* to start with.

Tool 5: Commitment of time

All the tools available are to no avail without a commitment of time and a commitment to concentration. Meditation takes time. We seem to have the time to do what we want but not the time to do what we should. Consistency in spending extended periods of time in God's Word is a key to proper meditation. Anytime is a good time, but if you give God, say, one-half hour every morning before you get pulled into your fast and furious daily routine, you will actually wake up in the morning looking forward to spending that time with God. (By the way, if you think you are too busy, consider that this kind of meditation in God's Word will simply replace the wasted time it takes to sin.)

Tool 6: A set place

Finding the right place to ensure complete concentration is also a must. Unless you have a set place to meditate, distractions can easily cause your mind to drift. Find a place where you are isolated, or at least insulated, from the distractions of TV, newspapers, radio, children, friends, and weariness. Find a place where it is just you and God and it is almost like the whole world disappears for those few minutes each morning.

Tool 7: Prayer

Talk to God. Ask God to open your eyes and your heart to what He is saying. Ask God for wisdom; He promises to give it to you. Ask God for understanding; He wants you to understand. Ask God for insight into His heart. Ask God to help you think as He thinks, to look at sin as He looks at sin, to love kindness and forgiveness as He loves kindness and forgiveness. Your goal is to defeat the anger in your heart by having the mind of Christ. When your meditation becomes your mindset, you will be amazed at your understanding of Scripture and your progress in consistent victory over selfish, sinful thinking. You'll also be pleasing God and not self.

Before we step into the heart of this book, let's walk through one short passage using the tools mentioned above. What is God saying to us in Proverbs 5:22? What words do we need to study and understand so that we do not miss their meaning and intent? What word pictures do these words bring to mind that will help us not only fully understand what they are saying but also apply in such a way that they evoke a stronger love for God and a more intense hatred for sin?

This is what God says.

Proverbs 5:22
His own iniquities shall take the wicked himself, and he shall be holden with the cords of his sins.

Now think about it.

Who is *his*, *himself*, *he*, and *his* referring to? (This is where you look at the sentence grammatically to find out who these personal pronouns are referring to. This one is easy. They are all pointing to a wicked person.) A wicked, sinful, selfish person. A person just like you and me! What are iniquities and sins? (Studying your Strong's concordance or a Bible dictionary will reveal not only that iniquity is sin but also that in the Old Testament it has the concept of worthless or nothing—a moral worthlessness. It is foolish, vain, and worthless and does absolutely nothing good for your life and relationship with God. Those involved in iniquity are simply wasting their lives away. Sin is defiant rebellion against God. It is choosing your way above God's way. It is making a god of yourself, worshiping yourself, putting yourself in an esteemed position above the true God.)

What are the words *take*, *holden*, and *cords* referring to? The word *take* according to Strong's means "to catch in a net, a trap or a pit; to capture." The word *holden* means "to keep or to restrain." *Cords* are best described as something that is intertwined as a noose or ropes that confine or shackle. Put these three words together and you think of either a hunter trying to trap game, a medieval enemy seeking to capture and imprison slaves in a damp, dark dungeon, or a life of imprisonment as a wicked criminal behind bars. All three examples involve captivity or servitude. These word pictures help us to understand and apply this simple verse.

How can this affect me?

Who wants to be entrapped and destroyed like a wild animal? Who would volunteer to be the slave of a selfish, lying, uncaring master? Who wants to be treated like an imprisoned criminal? Who wants to spend the rest of his life in prison, separated from his wife and children, forgotten by his friends and coworkers, surrounded by ungodly, angry men who have experimented and perfected every sinful perversion imaginable with their depraved minds? The answer? The person who allows his anger to control him. The guy who abuses those he is supposed to love through his rage and fury. Do you really want to be a slave to sin for the rest of your life?

The more you meditate, the better you will become at meditation.

The more you meditate, the better you will become at meditation. It really does not take too long to become somewhat of a pro. After a while, you will find yourself simply reading a passage as your mind begins to race with synonyms, word pictures, explanations, applications, and illustrations. Your meditation toolbox will gradually fill with your favorite tools, whether they live on your bookshelf or hide on the hard drive of your computer. Your understanding, teaching, preaching, counseling, and everyday life fellowshiping will be enriched by your grasp of God's Word.

The rest of this book will simply illustrate and give examples of the application of the mechanics of meditation. May we all agree with what David shared in Psalm 119:97, "O how love I thy law! It is my meditation all the day."

Meditation 1

Do you really want to look so foolish?

This is what God says.

Ecclesiastes 7:9

Be not hasty in thy spirit to be angry: for anger resteth in the bosom of fools.

Now think about it.

Don't be hasty in your spirit, eager in your heart, or rash in your thinking to be angry. Anger is one sin that feels right at home in the hearts of foolish, unreasonable, selfish men; it rests in the bosom of fools.

How can this affect me?

God calls quick-tempered, short-fused, explosive individuals fools. Do you want to know what God thinks when you lose your temper and scream at your children? He thinks you are acting very foolishly. Do you wonder about God's view of those who quickly fly off the handle at the slightest provocation? God thinks they are acting like fools. God looks at teens who lash out at their brothers, sisters, or parents in fits of rage as very foolish young people. It is not that an angry man cannot think; he foolishly chooses not to think. He is obstinate. An angry fool has the propensity to make stupid choices that hurt everyone who really cares about him. A fool's anger leads to a life of destruction. What a terrible way to live.

This is what God says.

Proverbs 14:17

He that is soon angry dealeth foolishly: and a man of wicked devices is hated.

Now think about it.

Anyone who is hot-tempered, quick to be angry, or loses his temper at the slightest provocation acts like a fool; and those who scheme, plot, and plan how they can use their outbursts of anger and manipulative wrath to fulfill their wicked intentions are hated by everyone.

How can this affect me?

Angry individuals are blind to how stupid they really look! They think that their out-of-control raging will so intimidate and manipulate those around them that they will be able to have their own way. Crazy people repeat the same actions over and over regardless of the consequences. Angry men are crazy. Foolish! Most adults will laugh out

It is not easy to love an angry man.

loud at a small child kicking and screaming his way through a temper tantrum. Most young people laugh inside at moms and dads who threaten and scream their way through their own temper tantrums. Screaming is foolish. Yelling is foolish. Slamming doors is foolish. Throwing furniture and frying pans is foolish. Cursing is foolish. Uncontrolled anger is foolish. Those who believe that their manipulative anger will give them the control they demand are only fooling themselves. It is not easy to love an angry man. It is difficult not to be bitter against an angry parent. One sure consequence of anger is hate. No one wants to hate anyone, but the fear caused by constant yelling and screaming pushes those attacked to respond in hatred. Those who are quick to be angry are foolishly driving away those who would normally love them.

This is what God says.

Proverbs 14:29
He that is slow to wrath is of great understanding:
but he that is hasty of spirit exalteth folly.

Now think about it.

The individual who is patient does not easily get mad, is not quick to fly off the handle, and takes a long, slow breath before responding in wrath is incredibly wise and has discretion and understanding; but the one who is impatient, lacking in character, and hasty of spirit exalts the fact that he is thick-headed, stupid, and foolish.

How can this affect me?

How long does it take for you to explode in anger? Are you a slow-burner or a flame-thrower? Do you turn up the heat right away or do you allow yourself time to think before you react? Are you thankful that God is not as quick-tempered as you sometimes are? "The Lord is merciful and gracious, slow to anger, and plenteous in mercy" (Ps. 103:8). "The Lord is gracious, and full of compassion; slow to anger, and of great mercy" (Ps. 145:8). "The Lord is slow to anger, and great in power, and will not at all acquit the wicked: the Lord hath his way in the whirlwind and in the storm, and the clouds are the dust of his feet" (Nah. 1:3). Those who know God know that He is patient, longsuffering, and slow to anger. What do those who know you think about the way you deal with your anger? The way you handle your anger determines how others perceive you. You are known for your patience or impatience, wisdom or foolishness, understanding or stupidity, slow response or quick reaction, out-of-control anger or under-control calm. How are you perceived by your family? Your friends? Your coworkers? Your Lord?

Meditation 2

Don't you care how much you are hurting those you love with your anger?

This is what God says.

Proverbs 27:3–4

A stone is heavy, and the sand weighty; but a fool's wrath is heavier than them both. Wrath is cruel, and anger is outrageous; but who is able to stand before envy?

Now think about it.

A stone is heavy, hard to carry, and incredibly burdensome, and sand is weighty, difficult to lift off the ground without causing excessive pain and weariness; but a fool's wrath, his provoking spirit that leads to exasperation, grief, and vexation of the heart is more difficult to pick up, is more burdensome to carry, is heavier than both the weighty sand and the heavy stone. Wrath (intensely hot anger revealed in rage or fury) is cruel, insensitive, and devoid of any compassion. Anger (the visible rage seen in furrowed brows, red faces, and hateful eyes) is as outrageous as an overwhelming flood and as devastating as a life-threatening tsunami. But who is able to stand firm without being knocked over or swept away with hostile, passionate envy that locks your heart on something or someone God never intended you to have?

How can this affect me?

Often the burdens we carry in life are self-imposed. The heavy hearts and hopeless weights we drag around are simply consequences of our unwillingness to confess and forsake the wrath and anger that control us. We drag our feet through life burdened with frustration, irritation, and edginess. There is a constant fear of looking like a fool because of outbursts of anger and volcanic eruptions of wrath. We fill our backpacks with more rocks and sand every time we scream at our children, argue with our mates, stonewall our parents, and shake our heads in disgust at God. The burden gets almost too heavy to carry, and it is our own fault! Although our wrath and anger are aimed to hurt others, they work as a spiritual boomerang that quickly comes back to hurt us. It is foolish to carry around such anger. Either empty your pack or let the weight of it pull you to the ground. Empty your backpack of stone-heavy anger by simply admitting the foolishness of your sin to God. Turn your pack upside down and shake every bit of wrath out of it by confessing your sin to those who have personally felt the heaviness of your rage. If you don't confess, forsake, and empty your heart of wrath and anger, you will not be able to stand. The weight of your sin will overcome you. You will fall.

This is what God says.

Ephesians 6:4
And, ye fathers, provoke not your children to wrath: but bring them up in the nurture and admonition of the Lord.

Now think about it.

Dads, do not provoke your children to wrath, do not enrage them, do not irritate them, do not frustrate them to the point of resentment; do not exasperate them until they blow up in anger; instead, help them through disciplined training, encourage them with loving instruction, raise your children (bring them up) in the nurture and instructive admonition the Lord approves of and is pleased with.

How can this affect me?

Most parents (especially dads) are either hot or cold. They get it or they don't. Parents either drive their children away with their destructive anger or draw them closer with their loving instruction. This is very confusing for children and teens. One day they are being praised and blessed, and the next day they are being cut down and cursed. James said, "Out of the same mouth proceedeth blessing and cursing. My brethren, these things ought not so to be." Dads, if you brag on your children on Monday and then blast them off the face of the earth on Tuesday, you are in sin! This type of selfish behavior "ought not to be." Stop it! Quit allowing your personal frustrations to provoke them. It is hard for children to be smothered in inconsistency, wondering when they wake up in the morning whether they will be treated with loving instruction or exasperating hostility. Bring them up; don't tear them down. Allow your children the joy and confidence of consistent and constant Bible-based instruction. Provide an atmosphere of spiritual growth. Draw them close to you with the loving encouragement that pleases God rather than drive them away with the discouraging anger that pleases self. Get rid of your anger. Just love your children!

This is what God says.

Colossians 3:21
Fathers, provoke not your children to anger, lest they be discouraged.

Now think about it.

Dads, do not aggravate your children, do not provoke your children into arguments, do not make them angry with your quarrelling, fighting, and contention.

If you do, they will get discouraged, lose heart, become apathetic, and quit trying.

How can this affect me?

Dads can provoke their children in a number of ways, as revealed in the different Greek words translated *provoke* in Scripture. In Ephesians 6:4 *provoke* means to arouse to wrath, to exasperate and infuriate. It is a provocation that leads to rage. In Colossians 3:21 *provoke* results in arguing, quarrelling, and contention. Even though there may be times of disagreement and discussion, dads are never to argue with their children. Some dads seem to get a thrill out of getting their families to argue with them so they can proudly prove their families wrong and themselves right. Arguing, contention, and strife steal the passion out of a child's heart. A fifteen-year-old girl once told me, "My dad attacks my character and threatens my life. I just have to tune him out." Another thirteen-year-old girl shared with me, "My parents are very angry people. There isn't a day that goes by that someone does not end up crying or yelling. It hurts! My parents just got a divorce. I've known pain all my life, but nothing has been worse than this.

Crying, yelling, depression, and bitterness have invaded what used to be a happy home." Parents wonder why young people today are plagued with apathy. If they would just stop to listen to themselves for a minute, they would see where the apathy comes from. Constant strife is discouraging to any child. Arguing disheartens children. These children, facing what should be maturity in their parents, view only the foolishness and immaturity of their parents' wrath and anger. The same young people who feel they cannot please their parents and only make them mad believe it is impossible to ever please God. So why try? Give up! Let the passion and zeal disappear. Thanks, mom and dad.

Meditation 3

Anger says, "Don't tell me I'm wrong!"

This is what God says.

Proverbs 21:24

Proud and haughty scorner is his name, who dealeth in proud wrath.

Now think about it.

A man who is proud and haughty should be given the nickname "Scorner" or "Scoffer." He is known for his overwhelming pride, his boundless arrogance, and his out-of-control wrath.

How can this affect me?

Angry people are riddled with pride. If arrogance were a disease, it would result in a "Swiss cheesing" of an angry person's heart. Angry individuals such as Mr. Pride, Dr. Haughty, Mrs. Scorner, and Miss Mocker view themselves quite differently than those who know them well. They are blinded to the way they are seen through the eyes of their family and friends. They would be shocked in disbelief if they realized how God sees their anger as such foolishness. Proud people think they are never wrong! They avoid confrontation and anyone who may have the courage to correct them. Those who are often proud and easily angered are true biblical scorners. They scorn anyone who disagrees with them. They scoff at any teaching that would prove them wrong. They mock preachers and leaders in an effort to divert the convicting truth that could uncover their wicked haughtiness. Solomon tells us that "the scorner is an abomination to men." The angry scorner in his blinding pride drives everyone away. He is disliked by all. While his pride may be concealed behind a countenance that depicts that everything is

Proud people think they are never wrong!

fine, in reality, his heart is broken because he knows he is hated by many. Solomon also instructs us to "cast out the scorner and contention shall go out; yea, strife and reproach shall cease." Nobody wants an arrogant person around. Those who are in love with themselves will soon have only themselves to love.

This is what God says.

Ephesians 4:31–32

Let all bitterness, and wrath, and anger, and clamour, and evil speaking, be put away from you, with all malice: and be ye kind one to another, tenderhearted, forgiving one another, even as God for Christ's sake hath forgiven you.

Now think about it.

It is time to get rid of all bitterness (the deep-seated anger that refuses to be reconciled), all wrath and anger (explosive rage and hot tempers), all clamor and evil speaking (argumentative, harsh words and malicious slander), along with all malice (evil intent); instead, replace those hateful acts of selfishness with kindness, tenderheartedness, and forgiveness—the same kindness, tenderheartedness, and forgiveness that God (for Christ's sake) has given you.

How can this affect me?

Someone has said that you can't teach an old dog new tricks. Many use this saying as an excuse. "I don't have to change. I can't change. This is just the way I am!" It may be the way you are, but it is not the way you have to be for the rest of your life! And speaking of old dogs, this passage of Scripture was written not to vicious dogs but to angry people. New tricks? These are not tricks but commands of God to change our angry hearts to be like the kind, tenderhearted, forgiving heart of Jesus Christ. How did we get so angry and bitter in the first place? Usually, someone said something that offended us. Then he did something that hurt us even more. We probably misread or misunderstood what was said or done; nevertheless, we allowed the ugly sin of malice to crawl its way into our hearts. Once we were intent to get back at the person, once we set our minds to make him hurt as much as he made us hurt, we followed the all-too-common progression of destructive, ungodly communication. It started with a seed of bitterness that quickly grew into outbursts of anger and fits of rage. Then we purposefully shouted harsh and cutting words aimed at hurting and slandering the ones we were attacking. God tells us to stop! Get rid of such foolish behavior. Put these childish antics as far away from us as we can. Then what? Show kindness to the same people with which we were bitter. To those we attacked with rage and anger, we are to show tenderheartedness, that ability to see a hurting person and the willingness to do something about it. To the ones we slandered and cut down with our words, we are to use words that build up and encourage. To all, we are to forgive. You can't teach old dogs new tricks. But we are not dogs. We are not talking about tricks. We are to change to be like the forgiving God, Who has forgiven us.

This is what God says.

Colossians 3:19
Husbands, love your wives, and be not bitter against them.

Now think about it.

Husbands, love your wives with the same intensity that God loves you, and don't be bitter toward them or treat them harshly.

How can this affect me?

Men, what do you think about your wife? (If you are a wife, what is the first thing your husband thinks about you?) Is it how much you love her or how much she irritates you? Do you treat her with the same tenderness you did when you were first dating or do you attempt to control her spirit with harsh, unfeeling words and actions? Men, what is it that makes you bitter with your wife? Never let the things that irritate you (her laziness, her lateness, her looks, or her lack of intimacy) put a bitter taste in your mouth. Learn to overlook every weakness with the same love that God loves you.

Love her!

Love her with an unconditional love (Rom. 5:8).

Love her with an unquestioned love (John 3:16).

Love her with an unselfish love (Eph. 5:25).

Love her with an uninterrupted love (Rom. 8:38–39).

Love her with an unending love (John 13:1).

Love her . . . and don't be bitter.

Meditation 4

Like (angry) father, like (angry) son.

This is what God says.

Proverbs 22:24–25

Make no friendship with an angry man; and with a furious man thou shalt not go: lest thou learn his ways, and get a snare to thy soul.

Now think about it.

Do not become best friends with a hot-tempered, angry man; do not even associate with a furious, easily angered man; if you do, you will learn his ways and become just like him, entrapped in a life of selfish anger and foolish rage.

How can this affect me?

Angry people produce angry people. Anger is a contagious poison that quickly paralyzes patience, thoughtfulness, and understanding. Anger is a deadly disease that is transmitted by rubbing shoulders and hanging out with angry people. Angry dads infect angry sons. Angry moms produce angry daughters. Young children are highly susceptible to the contamination caused by angry brothers and sisters. Angry friends pass the disease on to their friends. Once anger gets into a home or a friendship, it spreads in epidemic proportions, contaminating everyone in its path. Unlike a twenty-four-hour virus, anger lingers and takes months and even years to flush out of the system. Once the anger encompasses the heart, it holds the individual in bondage to its deceitful desires. It redirects the contaminated individuals to walk down a path that leads away from those who really care and want to help. It destroys all relationships. Angry people produce angry people. A thirteen-year-old girl told me, "I live with an angry person—my

34

dad. He loses his temper all the time and I hate to ask my friends over for fear of embarrassment. This used to make me angry until I realized something. . . . I was the same way." Angry friends produce angry friends. Are you dating an angry person? Do you have angry friends? Are you an angry friend? Remember that God said, "Make no friendship with an angry man."

This is what God says.

Proverbs 18:6
A fool's lips enter into contention, and his mouth calleth for strokes.

Now think about it.

A fool is always looking for someone to argue with, his lips enter into contention and controversy, and his mouth calls for strokes (which, for most individuals, means they will receive the beating of their lives.)

How can this affect me?

Only by pride comes contention. A proud fool loves to show how great he is by arguing with women and picking fights with either children or smaller men he knows he can beat. He looks for controversy and begs for a fight. The foolishness of fighting has been on children's playgrounds for years. Often you hear angry kids say, "Come on, hit me! I dare you!" or "My dad can beat up your dad!" (I know some moms who can beat up some dads.) The childish fighting that is seen on playgrounds and in school halls should never be carried into our adult lives. It is a sign of gross immaturity. It is sad what anger can do to destroy children's lives.

An eighteen-year-old boy shared with me what it was like to live in an angry home.

"I live with two angry people. They are always fighting . . . if not with each other with me. It has gotten worse as I have gotten older. I'm the baby and all my brothers and sisters are gone so I'm the only one left to yell at. My dad can see a commercial on TV and find something to yell at me or my mom about. My mom yells so much she doesn't even realize when she is yelling anymore. The only person who even knows it is this bad is a friend of mine at church. When I was younger, my main function in life was to change the TV channel, but now he [my dad] has a remote, so all I do is go upstairs and lock the door to escape the constant fighting. One time it got so bad we got into a fistfight. My dad is 54, 6' 6" and 230 pounds. Then I hit the lowest point in my life. It turns out [in our fight] I broke my dad's jaw. The bad thing is when he couldn't fight back that was when I unloaded. He spent two days in the hospital and I spent a week in jail. That is why I had to come to a Christian school. The best thing about that, I got to start over."

No teen should have to live in a home with so much anger. Do you constantly argue and fight with others in your home? Remember, a proud fool is always looking for someone to argue with. Don't be such a fool.

This is what God says.

Proverbs 13:20
He that walketh with wise men shall be wise: but a companion of fools shall be destroyed.

Now think about it.

Those who walk, spend a lot of time, and live with wise men will become even wiser; but a companion of fools, a friend of foolish men who are known for their selfishness and anger, will harm themselves and destroy all hopes for strong, uplifting relationships with wise men.

How can this affect me?

Wisdom and foolishness seem to be contagious. The trait you catch is determined by whom you spend the most time with. There are definite paths and lifestyles chosen by the Wise family and the Foolish family. The Wise family attracts those who are kind, understanding, and tenderhearted to their way of living. The Foolish family is usually surrounded by those who are belligerent, unreasonable, and angry. The Wise children love having their friends over, while the Foolish children never invite anyone to their home in fear that they will be embarrassed by yet another explosion of foolish anger. The Wise family shares what they are learning with each other, while the Foolish family argues about what they think they know. The Wise listen; the Foolish talk. If you have visited either home, you probably know that you cannot wait to get to the Wise home and cannot wait to leave the Foolish home. After a few minutes, even a stranger can tell with whom you have been spending your time. Look at your group of friends. Who enjoys being around you? If they are wise, you have probably been an encouragement to them. If they are foolish, so are you.

Meditation 5

Those who often get mad, often go mad.

This is what God says.

Proverbs 17:12

Let a bear robbed of her whelps meet a man, rather than a fool in his folly.

Now think about it.

It would be safer for a man to meet a bear, or any raging beast robbed or bereaved of her cubs or little ones, than for him to meet a fool in the midst of his foolish outbursts of rage and anger.

How can this affect me?

Can you imagine the fear of being chased down and attacked by a ferocious grizzly bear who thought you were going to hurt her young cubs? You couldn't run fast enough or climb high enough to escape her destructive fury. She would tear you from limb to limb. Many of us have experienced the horror of being chased by an angry dog, but very few of us have faced the unleashed rage of a thousand-pound bear . . . or maybe you have! Solomon says that it would be safer to meet a bear than a foolish man or woman caught in a fit of rage. The bear's claw marks will heal with time; the emotional scars left by abusive parents, relatives, or even so-called friends do not heal so quickly. A thirteen-year-old girl shared, "I live with an angry mom. One time on my birthday, she whipped me with a curling iron cord. She always yells at everybody; it makes me feel like a nobody. I have learned just to shut my mouth and not talk back or say anything to make her mad." Another girl told me, "I have a mother that is angry. And sometimes when she

gets really mad she curses and hits me and slaps me."
Young people should not have to grow up this way, and
if they had their choice, they wouldn't. Most of them
would rather meet an angry bear in the woods than go
home to their mom and dad.

This is what God says.

Matthew 2:16

Then Herod, when he saw that he was mocked of
the wise men, was exceeding wroth, and sent forth,
and slew all the children that were in Bethlehem,
and in all the coasts thereof, from two years old and
under, according to the time which he had diligently inquired of the wise men.

Now think about it.

King Herod, when he saw that he was mocked and
outsmarted by the wise men, became furious and exceedingly angry. He literally lost his mind and went
mad. He sent soldiers to kill all the children that lived
around Bethlehem from two years old and under. (It
had been about two years since the wise men had asked
about the newborn king of the Jews.)

How can this affect me?

Anger and wrath can turn even a king into a madman. Uncontrolled anger is not far from insanity. Psychiatric hospital wards are filled with individuals who have never learned to control their rage. Their anger has made them mad. The word *mad* can be used in both cases. When we "get mad," we let down our guard and give in to our anger, allowing the fury to control everything we say and do. When we "go mad," we don't just give in, we give up. For those watching our insanity, there is not much difference between getting mad and going mad. They both magnify our selfishness, foolishness, and resistance to the Spirit of God. While pastoring, I held a tiny newborn in my arms and dedicated her to the Lord. The young parents had good intentions, but wrong friends led to wrong choices (including alcohol), causing the mom to hold her tiny baby by the feet and beat her into a wall just to get her to stop crying. The baby was rescued and fortunately survived. The mother went to prison. The insanity of foolish anger again raised up its ugly head in conquest over weak, foolish individuals. Would your children or spouse say that you are crazy? Would your parents or friends think you have gone mad? Would anyone who views your outbursts of anger recognize that you are insane? Insane madness is a scary thing. It causes great fear in the hearts of those involved. If you consistently get mad, you may eventually go mad. Don't be such a fool.

This is what God says.

Ecclesiastes 10:12–13

The words of a wise man's mouth are gracious; but the lips of a fool will swallow up himself. The beginning of the words of his mouth is foolishness: and the end of his talk is mischievous madness.

Now think about it.

The words of a wise man's mouth are gracious, kind, and encouraging (they give honor to the wise man). But a fool will destroy himself with his own lips; he will swallow himself up and literally eat himself alive. When a fool begins to speak, he bases his words on mere foolishness; when a fool ends what he has to say and finally concludes, his words reveal his wicked, mischievous, raving madness.

How can this affect me?

What you say reveals what you are. "For from within, out of the heart of men, proceed evil thoughts, adulteries, fornications, murders, thefts, covetousness, wickedness, deceit, lasciviousness, an evil eye, blasphemy, pride, foolishness: all these evil things come from within, and defile the man." The words of a wise person reveal his wisdom. The words of a fool reveal his foolishness. Have you ever said something in anger that you wish you could have taken back? Have you ever hurt someone close to you with what you said but then, in the frustration of the moment, were too upset or too proud to apologize? Do you think that those you attack with your words know you really don't mean what you say and hope they will get over it? If you think angry, cruel, harsh words are easily forgotten, you are crazy. If you think you do not need to ask forgiveness from a spouse, a child, or a friend for the mean things you have said, you are going mad. A test to see whether a person is crazy is to see if he repeats the same action over and over again with the same negative consequences. Some beat their heads against a wall. Some furiously rock back and forth in rocking chairs. Some talk to their dolls, waiting for the reply that will never come. Has your anger caused you to go mad? Do you repeat the same angry words toward your wife or husband knowing how upset it will make him? Do you scream at your children day after day, knowing that you are provoking them to wrath? Do you continue to get upset with your friends, clam up and pout, knowing that it just drives them farther away from you? If you repeat your anger, bitterness, selfishness, and foolishness over and over, you are crazy. You have gotten mad so often, you have now gone mad.

Meditation 6

It's hard to believe someone loves you when he or she is always angry with you.

This is what God says.

Galatians 5:14–15

For all the law is fulfilled in one word, even in this; Thou shalt love thy neighbour as thyself. But if ye bite and devour one another, take heed that ye be not consumed one of another.

Now think about it.

For all the law is fulfilled in one short, concise statement, and here it is: "Love your neighbour as yourself."

But if in anger, you constantly bite (attack) and devour (seek to destroy) one another, be careful that you do not consume each other with your anger and hate.

How can this affect me?

How often has a young teen girl picked up a daisy, plucked the petals, and said, "He loves me, he loves me not, he loves me, he loves me not"? There are many reasons that someone feels unloved, but fighting and vicious, angry attacks are at the top of the list. On a mission trip to Kenya, I sat on top of a Land Cruiser and watched a family of hyenas devour what looked to be the leg of a gazelle. It was quite gruesome. Not only did they rip and tear at the leg, but they yipped and attacked each other. Not much laughing or loving in that hyena family. Sad to say, it reminded me of many homes where angry parents and bitter children viciously attack each other with angry growls and cutting words. It is a lose-lose situation. Everybody attacks each other. Everybody gets hurt. Everybody angrily protects his little area of life and bares his teeth at anyone who tries to invade his privacy. Living with such anger is animalistic. It is the life of a brute beast that is consumed with its own desires and nothing else. As a selfish animal, it is totally ignorant of what love is and what love can do for any relationship. Love wants to forgive. Love wants to reconcile. Love wants to get along. Love wants the best **Love wants to be Christlike.** for others over itself. Love wants to be Christlike. We all have a choice. We can continue to bite and devour each other like hungry beasts, or we can choose to love each other like God loves us. Do you give those you should love any reason to question your love? Can anyone say about you, "He loves me, he loves me not, he loves me, he loves me not"?

This is what God says.

1 Corinthians 13:5
[Love] doth not behave itself unseemly, seeketh not her own, is not easily provoked, thinketh no evil.

Now think about it.

Love does not behave in an unseemly, rude, crude, insensitive, or inappropriate way; love does not self-ishly demand its own way in disregard of all others' feelings and emotions; love is not quick to be angry, is not irritable, is not easily provoked; love does not think evil of anyone. It keeps no records of when it has been wronged; it tries to see the good in others and does not angrily accuse or blame them for something they never said or did.

How can this affect me?

Unseemly, rude, and crude behavior by professing Christians can turn some people away from the gospel before they ever hear it. Selfish believers who lack patience and are easily provoked can set up a wall between unbelievers and Jesus Christ just by their unloving attitudes. Love draws others closer. Anger drives others away. Love and anger are quite incompatible. Even if you truly love the person you are angry with, your anger can cause that person to doubt your love. Just as love is described in 1 Corinthians 13:5, so anger is described as its opposite.

[Anger] behaves in an unseemly, rude, crude, insensitive, and inappropriate way; [anger] selfishly demands its own way in total disregard of all other's feelings and emotions; [anger] is quick to be irritable and easily provoked. [Anger] thinks evil of everyone; it keeps records of when it has been wronged; it tries to see the evil in others and angrily accuses and blames them for things they never said or did.

If you are an angry person, you are not a loving person. If you are known for your anger, you will probably not have much success in drawing others to Christ.

This is what God says.

Ephesians 4:1–2

I therefore, the prisoner of the Lord, beseech you that ye walk worthy of the vocation wherewith ye are called, with all lowliness and meekness, with longsuffering, forbearing one another in love.

Now think about it.

As a servant of the Lord (for which I am now in prison), I beg all Christians who have been called of God to live a life that pleases the Lord with humility and gentleness, lowliness and meekness, patience, and longsuffering, showing tolerance and making allowance for each other's faults and weaknesses because of your love.

How can this affect me?

It is easy to excuse our anger because of difficult circumstances and difficult people. In this passage, Paul was imprisoned for doing what is right! As a servant of God he was treated with everything but love, tolerance, patience, and humility. Yet he did not use his difficult situation as an excuse for selfishness, harshness, or impatience. He did not allow the harsh treatment he experienced in prison to make him angry. In the place of anger, he humbled himself. In the place of anger, he showed gentleness. In the place of anger, he remained patient. In the place of anger, he showed love. Anger is a choice. Love is a choice. We can come up with all the excuses in the world and give a hundred and one reasons for losing our patience and getting angry, but none of them please our Lord, Who called us to be His children. There is no excuse to be angry.

Meditation 7

No one can make you angry.
You choose to be angry.

This is what God says.

Genesis 4:5–7

But unto Cain and to his offering he had not respect. And Cain was very wroth, and his countenance fell. And the Lord said unto Cain, Why art thou wroth? and why is thy countenance fallen? If thou doest well, shalt thou not be accepted? and if thou doest not well, sin lieth at the door. And unto thee shall be his desire, and thou shalt rule over him.

Now think about it.

Even though God accepted Abel's offering, He did not look on Cain's offering with interest, respect, or favor. Because of this, Cain was very angry as his heart burned with intense wrath; his facial expression fell as he scowled in anger. The Lord asked Cain, "Why are you burning up with such intense anger? Why has your countenance fallen? Why do you look so angry? Why is that scowl on your face? If you do well, if you do what is right, if you do what you know you should do in regard to your sacrifice, didn't I tell you that your offering will be accepted? But remember, if you choose to go against what I have said and sacrifice your own way, sin (like a wild, hungry animal) is ready to pounce on you and tear you apart, limb by limb. Sin's desire is to control you. You had better take control of your sin before it takes control of you. If you don't kill it, it will kill you." God's approval is very important. God does not look on you with a casual or disinterested glance. He is interested in you and looks deep into your heart to determine the motives and desires behind your daily decisions. He wants you to do the same. When anger takes control of your heart, stop to ask yourself the same question that God asked Cain: "Why am I so angry?"

How can this affect me?

Why are you so angry? It is your choice. You don't have to be angry. In fact, you really have no reason or right to be upset. The only reason you are angry is that you choose to be angry. Ask yourself why. In fact, ask yourself five whys. If Cain had asked the five whys, he may have kept his anger from turning into murder. Imagine the following thought process that could have, and should have, been in Cain's mind.

Why am I so angry?

Because God did not accept my offering like He did Abel's.

Why does that make me so angry?

Because I want God to accept me just the way I am.

Why won't God accept my offering?

Because I wanted to sacrifice my own way.

Why is my way the wrong way and God's way the only way?

Because God sees my heart. He knows my motives.

Why don't I swallow my selfishness and pride and choose to please God instead of pleasing myself?

Because . . . because . . . I don't know. Maybe I should!

Anger is a choice. I cannot blame my anger on anyone or anything but myself. When I am angry, it is because I choose to be so.

This is what God says.

1 Timothy 6:3–4

If any man teach otherwise, and consent not to wholesome words, even the words of our Lord Jesus Christ, and to the doctrine which is according to godliness; he is proud, knowing nothing, but doting about questions and strifes of words, whereof cometh envy, strife, railings, evil surmisings. Perverse disputings of men of corrupt minds, and destitute of the truth, supposing that gain is godliness: from such withdraw thyself.

Now think about it.

If anyone cannot agree with the simple, wholesome words of our Lord Jesus Christ, and argues with what the Bible teaches about having a godly life, he is arrogant, proud, and incredibly selfish. Even though he thinks he knows it all, he really knows nothing. He is conceited and ignorant. He dotes. He has a strange desire to change the meaning of words, has an unhealthy interest in arguing about what words really mean, is argumentative, and loves controversy. Such foolishness results in arguments that cause envy and jealousy, strife and fighting, malicious talk, hurtful gossip, vindictive slander and verbal abuse, false suspicions and evil accusations, constant friction, useless wrangling and perverse disputings. This foolishness comes from trouble-making men whose minds do not think right or function properly, corrupt minds that are totally destitute of the truth. They are depraved in their minds and deprived of the truth. They think religion is just a way to get rich. Their motives for godliness are all messed up. God says to stay away from such angry, argumentative, divisive people.

How can this affect me?

Angry people love to argue. Their pride keeps them from admitting that they might be wrong and someone else (even God) might be right. They choose to be stupid! They love to debate, but the minute they see they could be proved wrong, they switch from logical reasoning to emotional manipulation. They begin to change the meaning of words to cover their ignorance. They attack the character of people rather than search for solutions to problems. They get mad! As they begin to lose control of the discussion, their obvious lack of understanding forces them to seek some other way to stay in control of the situation. They explode! Their tirade causes those who actually see the biblical solution for the problem to back off and let the explosive arguers have their temper tantrums. No one wants to be around such people. In fact, even God tells us to quietly leave the situation. Anger is a choice. So is looking stupid.

This is what God says.

Romans 2:6–11

Who will render to every man according to his deeds: to them who by patient continuance in well doing seek for glory and honour and immortality, eternal life: but unto them that are contentious, and do not obey the truth, but obey unrighteousness, indignation and wrath, tribulation and anguish, upon every soul of man that doeth evil, of the Jew first, and also of the Gentile; but glory, honour, and peace, to every man that worketh good, to the Jew first, and also to the Gentile: for there is no respect of persons with God.

Now think about it.

God does not play favorites. He is fair and will give to everyone what he or she has worked so hard for. He will give eternal life to those who have trusted in Him and patiently seek for the glory, honor, and immortality He promises. He will give His indignation, wrath, tribulation, and anguish to those who selfishly seek their own way, insist on living an evil life, and reject the truth of God's Word. God does not play favorites. He is no respecter of persons. Whether you are a Jew or a Gentile, rich or poor, popular or unpopular, talented or boring, if you do what is right, if you do good, God will bless you with glory, honor, and peace.

How can this affect me?

You get what you ask for. You earn what you work for. Whether good or evil, you will be rewarded according to how you labor. You do have a choice in the matter and your choice is quite simple. You can have a heart full of peace or a heart torn with anguish. You can have honor or indignation. You can be respected by men or hated by men. You can have God's blessing or God's wrath. You can have the hope of eternal life or the fear of eternal death. You can be controlled by the spirit of anger or controlled by the Spirit of God. It is your choice.

Meditation 8

Anger is a form of premeditated murder.

This is what God says.

Matthew 5:21–24

Ye have heard that it was said by them of old time, Thou shalt not kill; and whosoever shall kill shall be in danger of the judgment: but I say unto you, that whosoever is angry with his brother without a cause shall be in danger of the judgment: and whosoever shall say to his brother, Raca, shall be in danger of the council: but whosoever shall say, Thou fool, shall be in danger of hell fire. Therefore if thou bring thy gift to the altar, and there rememberest that thy brother hath ought against thee; leave there thy gift before the altar, and go thy way; first be reconciled to thy brother, and then come and offer thy gift.

Now think about it.

You have heard what God told His people hundreds of years ago in Exodus 20:13, "Do not commit murder" and "Whoever commits murder is guilty before the courts of law." But I tell you that everyone who is angry with his brother is just as guilty; and anyone who says to his brother, Raca "you good-for-nothing idiot," is guilty enough to be brought before the Sanhedrin, the highest council, similar to the Supreme Court; but whoever says, "You fool," is guilty enough to spend eternity in the fire of hell. Therefore, if you bring your gift to the altar, you come to worship your Lord, and there you remember that your brother has something against you; stop worshiping, leave your gift at the altar, and find your brother and be reconciled to him. Then after you know you are right with your brother and the Lord, come and worship your Lord and offer your gift.

How can this affect me?

Did you catch what Jesus is saying here? Being guilty of anger is just as bad as being guilty of murder? How could He say that? Wouldn't it be better to hate your brother than to kill him? Wouldn't it be safer to cut him down with words than to stab him in the back with a knife? Why is the sin of anger just as bad in God's eyes as the sin of murder? As you meditate on these questions, try to think like God. We are quick to judge behavior and actions. God's omniscience enables Him to judge motives and the heart. Some people get so angry they lose all sense and will do anything . . . even murder . . . to get their own way. The first step to murder is anger. Have you ever watched a young child get so angry with another that he yelled out, "I hate you and I wish you were dead"? If that young child had the means and the method, he may have attempted murder. Why? Because the motive was already established in his immature heart. Intense anger mixed with immaturity (or alcohol and drugs) is the root cause of many murders. Whom do you hate? Who makes you incredibly angry or bitter every time you think of him? With such murderous hatred in your heart, you cannot properly worship your Lord, pray to your Lord, or even live for your Lord until the anger has been confessed and forsaken. Stop reading this book. Change your schedule for the day and find those you have been angry with and ask both them and God for forgiveness. When you are done and the relationships have been reconciled, then worship your Lord with a pure heart. Don't let anger kill you.

This is what God says.

Daniel 2:12–13

For this cause the king was angry and very furious, and commanded to destroy all the wise men of Babylon. And the decree went forth that the wise men should be slain; and they sought Daniel and his fellows to be slain.

Now think about it.

Because none of the astrologers, wise men, and soothsayers could come up with the forgotten dream that troubled Nebuchadnezzar, he became intensely angry and very furious. His anger prevented him from thinking clearly, evidenced by his command to execute all the wise men in Babylon. So the decree went forth that the wise men should be murdered; and they began searching for Daniel and his God-fearing friends to kill them.

How can this affect me?

King Nebuchadnezzar was the King of Anger. Nebuchadnezzar recognized no authority or law above himself. With absolutely no restraints to hold him back, he gave full vent to his anger and fury and sentenced to death those who irritated him, frustrated him, and disappointed him. He was so full of himself that he justified his furious anger. The justification of his anger gave evidence that he believed that killing the wise men would not be his fault and those who caused his anger were deserving of death. If you are so angry with someone that you wish he were dead, then you, like King Nebuchadnezzar, are in your heart guilty of premeditated murder. Do you justify your anger? Do you blame others for making you angry? Do you put yourself above all authority? Do you think you are an exception to what God has to say about selfish anger in His Word? If so, then you can join the ranks of wrathful royalty with King Nebuchadnezzar and also become a king of anger.

This is what God says.

Genesis 4:8
And Cain talked with Abel his brother: and it came to pass, when they were in the field, that Cain rose up against Abel his brother, and slew him.

Now think about it.

Later, after God had confronted Cain about his anger, Cain said to his brother Abel, "Let's go out to the field." While they were in the field, Cain, refusing to handle his anger God's way, attacked and killed his brother Abel.

How can this affect me?

Someone has said that sin will take you further than you want to go, keep you longer than you want to stay, and cost you more than you want to pay. Unbridled anger can result in utter destruction. If you are mad enough to scream at those you love, if you are mad enough to hurt those you care about, if you are mad enough to abuse those you are supposed to protect, you are a perfect candidate for murder. Angry thoughts aim the gun; murderous thoughts pull the trigger. If you think you can stop your fit of rage before you kill somebody, why can't you stop it before you hurt somebody? Angry people are one step away from becoming murderers. You had better reevaluate how you handle your anger. Your anger will take you further than you want to go, keep you longer than you want to stay, and cost you more than you want to pay.

This is what God says.

1 John 3:11–12

For this is the message that ye heard from the beginning, that we should love one another. Not as Cain, who was of that wicked one, and slew his brother. And wherefore slew he him? Because his own works were evil, and his brother's righteous.

Now think about it.

The Bible states a clear message from the beginning of Genesis to the end of Revelation that we should love one another. Don't be like Cain, who belonged to the Devil, Satan, that Wicked One, and murdered his own brother. Why did he kill him? Because Cain had been in sin, living in wickedness, doing evil, and his brother had chosen to do right. That made Cain angry, angry enough to kill.

How can this affect me?

Have you ever been angry enough to kill? Have you ever allowed anger to get such a hold of you that you physically abused your wife, your children, a brother, or a sister? Have you ever struck someone in anger? Have you ever been so mad that you wanted to destroy someone? If you had to say yes to any of these questions and you are continuing to live under the domination of such anger, then you are "of your father the devil, and the lusts of your father ye will do. He was a murderer from the beginning." Some statistics state that over twenty-five thousand murders are committed in the United States every year. Add to that the number of suicides (people murdering themselves) and abortion (the brutal murdering of unborn babies), and the statistics are staggering. Hardly a day goes by that local news does not report a murder. Cain would have made the headlines on CNN, ABC, CBS, NBC, and FOX News. What is the difference between you and Cain? Is it just that you have not acted on your murderous desires? Is it that you have not had the opportunity? Is it that you are too afraid that you could never get away with it? Or is it that you know your anger is wicked and evil, selfish and sinful, and you must kill it before it kills you . . . or kills someone you love? The only difference between Cain and many angry men and women is that Cain acted out what his heart felt. If your heart is just like Cain's, but you have not yet acted upon it, you had better change your heart before your anger changes you.

Meditation 9

Defensive anger becomes offensive anger.

This is what God says.

Proverbs 25:23–24

The north wind driveth away rain: so doth an angry countenance a backbiting tongue. It is better to dwell in the corner of the housetop, than with a brawling woman and in a wide house.

Now think about it.

Just like the north wind brings sudden rain seemingly out of nowhere, so does a nagging gossip, by her sly, critical, backbiting tongue, bring both angry and hurtful looks (so hurtful that the one attacked turns or hides his face from the attacker, thereby breaking communication). It would be better to live alone in a squatter's shack built in the corner of the housetop than to share a huge, beautiful home with an angry, contentious, nagging, argumentative, brawling woman.

How can this affect me?

Do you live in a big house? Is it big enough for those you hurt and offend with your angry, verbal attacks to run and hide? Do you live in a beautiful house? So beautiful that it would not only make the cover of *House Beautiful* but would also be the envy of most of the homeowners in your town? So beautiful that everyone would love to live there? Well, maybe not everyone. There are those who would rather live in a tiny shack or a small room in the attic than to put up with the critical, vicious contempt they experience in that big, beautiful house. It takes more than a house to make a home. It usually depends on how anger is handled that determines whether teens want to come "home" or can't wait to get out of the "house." Just like a strong northern wind drives away rain, so angry, bitter parents drive away their children. An angry, bitter wife drives away her husband in the same way. She may still have her big, beautiful house, but it will be a big, beautiful, *empty* house.

This is what God says.

Proverbs 21:19
It is better to dwell in the wilderness, than with a contentious and an angry woman.

Now think about it.

It is better to live alone in the wilderness on the backside of the desert, than to live with an angry, contentious, crabby, complaining wife.

How can this affect me?

It is better to live alone as a desert nomad than to marry an angry woman. It would be better to daily endure unbearable temperatures exceeding one hundred degrees than to live your life with an angry, contentious wife. It would be better to see nothing but sand dunes, mirages, and the blazing sun than to be committed to an angry, contentious, crabby woman. It would be better to go months at a time seeing only a desert lizard or a raw-boned vulture than to live in the same house with an angry, contentious, nagging, complaining wife. Could it be that your anger drives others away? Could it be that your husband sometimes wishes he could live as a desert nomad just to get away from you? Are you angry? Are you contentious? Are you crabby? Are you a complaining woman? If you are, and continue to be, you may someday replace your anger and contention with loneliness and misery. Don't drive those you love to the desert.

This is what God says.

Proverbs 27:15–16

A continual dropping in a very rainy day and a contentious woman are alike. Whosoever hideth her hideth the wind, and the ointment of his right hand, which bewrayeth itself.

Now think about it.

A contentious, argumentative, quarrelsome wife is as irritating and annoying as a constant dripping on a very rainy day. Trying to stop her nagging complaints and self-focused arguments is like trying to keep the wind from blowing or like firmly holding onto a heavy object with greasy hands.

How can this affect me?

Drip. Drip. Drip. Drip. Drip. Drip. The constant dripping of a leaky faucet or a damaged rain gutter can literally drive you crazy. "You're wrong; I'm right!" "You're wrong; I'm right!" "You're wrong; I'm right!" "You're wrong; I'm right!" The constant arguing and daily contention can cause you to go mad. A man who lives with an angry wife often gives up trying. He figures it would be easier to lasso a cyclone or pick up a greased watermelon than to get his wife to deal with her anger. Men cannot change their wives. But God can. Men just hear the constant drip, drip, drip, drip. But God, Who controls the wind with one hand and can hold the sun, moon, and stars in place with the other, can change the heart of an angry, contentious woman. Which would you rather face every day of your life—a wife who seeks to change to Christlikeness or the constant, irritating dripping of a complaining, angry wife?

Meditation 10

You can choose your anger, but you cannot choose the consequences of your anger.

This is what God says.

Genesis 4:10–14

And he said, What hast thou done? the voice of thy brother's blood crieth unto me from the ground. And now art thou cursed from the earth, which hath opened her mouth to receive thy brother's blood from thy hand; when thou tillest the ground, it shall not henceforth yield unto thee her strength; a fugitive and a vagabond shalt thou be in the earth. And Cain said unto the Lord, My punishment is greater than I can bear. Behold, thou hast driven me out this day from the face of the earth; and from thy face shall I be hid; and I shall be a fugitive and a vagabond in the earth; and it shall come to pass, that every one that findeth me shall slay me.

Now think about it.

The Lord spoke specifically to Cain asking, "What have you done? I can hear the shrieking cry for judgment and justice from Abel's blood. Cain, you murdered your brother. You are now cursed, bound with My very words, and banned from the productivity of the earth, which tasted your brother's blood, the blood that came directly from your angry, murderous hand. No matter how hard you work and toil, when you plow and cultivate the ground, it will not yield its strength and productivity like it used to. You will wander around the earth like a hunted fugitive and a homeless vagabond outside of any protective law. Cain, you are cursed. Because you refused to control your hateful anger and murderous fury, your life will be miserable." Cain then said to the Lord, "My punishment is too great to bear. The consequences of my choices are unfair. I did not know that the result of my anger would turn out this way. You have banished me from the land that is my life and hidden me from Your very presence and protection. I will now have to live like a wandering fugitive and a homeless vagabond. I know that the day will come that whoever finds me will kill me. Everyone will hate me and want to destroy me. My punishment is too great. I did not know it would end up this way. This is not fair!"

How can this affect me?

You can choose your sin, but you cannot choose the consequences of your sin. You can choose your anger, but you cannot choose the consequences of your anger. God told Cain that if he chose to do right, He would bless him. Instead, Cain listened to his anger rather than to God and chose to let that heart attitude explode into a murderous action. You say, "How could Cain do that? How could he hear the very voice of Almighty God and still kill his brother?" Just as God instructed Cain, He has also told you what to do with your anger. "Be angry, and sin not! Let every man be swift to hear, slow to speak, slow to wrath. Cease from anger!" Are you going to choose to deal with your anger God's way or, like Cain, give full vent to your anger and lash out in murderous rage with your words and actions? It is your choice. You can choose right now whether to react in anger. You can choose your anger but not the consequences. Cain believed that God was being unfair. Cain disagreed with the way God dealt with his fury. God didn't make Cain a wandering fugitive; Cain did that to himself. A normal consequence of anger is that you drive everyone away from you. Because of your volcanic explosions of wrath, those you are closest to are driven away. When they are young, they simply run to their rooms and cry on their beds. When they are older, they walk out of your life, refusing to allow your selfish, childish anger to hurt them anymore. You become a fugitive and a vagabond from your own family members. Your wife, husband, children, and grandchildren don't even want to be around you. If you think everyone is being unfair to you, just remember that

Anger drives everyone away.

you chose these consequences. If you think the people around you should just forgive and forget, they probably have forgiven, but it is not so easy to forget. Anger results in loneliness. Anger results in separation. Anger results in heartache. Anger results in misery. If this punishment is too great for you to bear, you had better choose to change your sinful anger because you cannot choose your consequences. You can choose your sin, but you cannot choose the consequences of your sin.

This is what God says.

Proverbs 19:19
A man of great wrath shall suffer punishment: for if thou deliver him, yet thou must do it again.

Now think about it.

A harsh, hot-tempered, short-fused, wrathful man will receive the punishment, pay the penalty, and suffer the consequences of his excessive wrath; if you rescue him from his punishment, pay his penalty for him, and deliver him from the consequences of his wrath, he will never learn and his habitual anger will surface again; then you will have to get him out of trouble again, he will get angry again, you'll need to help him again, ad nauseam.

How can this affect me?

Some people never learn. They are more concerned about the consequences of sin than the sin itself. They want to ride their little "anger train" without having to pay the fare. They want to keep their anger, but they want everyone else to forgive them. They want to maintain their rage, but they want their family to cover up for them and act as though nothing happened. They want to continue their selfish outbursts, but they don't want anyone to know that in a fit of rage they beat their wives black and blue. They enjoy the deceitful control they receive in the midst of their fury, but they refuse to think about their small children huddling in a corner in fear of being slapped or beaten. They want to explode but do not want to say they are sorry and ask for forgiveness. They want to verbalize their anger in screams and cursing but pretend it never happened. They want to crash through the house in a fury, smashing everything and everyone in sight, instilling lifelong fear in the hearts of their family, but they don't want that ten-year-old daughter to call 911, fearing that her daddy is going to hurt her mommy. They want their sin but not the consequences. They will destroy their own life and the lives of those they are supposed to love. They know their sinful anger is wrong, but they refuse to change. They don't seem to care! Some people will never learn.

This is what God says.

Proverbs 30:32–33

If thou hast done foolishly in lifting up thyself, or if thou hast thought evil, lay thine hand upon thy mouth. Surely the churning of milk bringeth forth butter, and the wringing of the nose bringeth forth blood: so the forcing of wrath bringeth forth strife.

Now think about it.

If you, through your pride and arrogance, have foolishly exalted yourself above everyone you know, or if you through your evil, wicked, selfish thinking have planned, plotted, and devised ways to make yourself look good and others look bad, hold your tongue, don't say a word, cover your mouth with your hand, and don't follow through with your proud plans. Why? Because just as surely as the constant churning and agitation of milk creates butter, and just as surely as the quick twisting of a person's nose results in a bloody nose, so both the constant irritation of a wrathful man and the quick, uncontrolled verbal attacks of an angry woman create strife, contention, arguing, quarreling, controversy, hurt feelings, proud spirits, and arrogant disagreements.

How can this affect me?

"Stop your fighting before somebody gets hurt!" Moms have been saying this to their sons and daughters for hundreds of years. The problem is, nobody listens. The children keep fighting and before long someone comes crying to mom because he got hurt. As the child sobs his way through the apparent injustice, Mom says, "I told you to stop fighting but you wouldn't listen!" Has God been trying to tell you Dad, Mom, Brother, or Sister to stop fighting? Has He not warned you that only by pride and selfishness come contention and fighting? God says as surely as milk will become butter if you constantly keep it churned and agitated, angry moms and dads will blow up if you constantly irritate them. They shouldn't, but they do. Angry people are weak people. Whatever is going on around them controls their spirit. You had better stop your fighting before someone gets hurt.

Meditation 11

Take a big breath, slow down, and think about what you are doing.

This is what God says.

James 1:19–20

Wherefore, my beloved brethren, let every man be swift to hear, slow to speak, slow to wrath: for the wrath of man worketh not the righteousness of God.

Now think about it.

My dear brothers and sisters, because of the patience you need to face temptation and the privilege you have had to receive the Word of truth, take note of everything that God has given you, and be quick to listen and swift to hear. Each one of us should be slow to speak and slow to get angry. Don't try to justify your anger, for there is absolutely no way that your anger can result in the righteous kind of life God wants you to live.

How can this affect me?

Are you quick to get angry? Do you have a short fuse? Do you blow up at the slightest provocation? Do you lose your temper at the snap of a finger? Slow down. Take a breath. Slow down. Listen for a moment. Slow down. Be careful what you say. Slow down. Think! Your anger will never accomplish God's best in your life or anyone else's life. Nothing is ever solved with selfish anger. Your anger can never justify the situation. Your anger can never make things right in the sight of God. Those who are quick to be angry only intensify the situation and make it worse. Slow down. Take a breath. Slow down. Listen for a moment. Slow down. Be careful what you say. Slow down. Think!

This is what God says.

Proverbs 19:11
The discretion of a man deferreth his anger; and it is
his glory to pass over a transgression.

Now think about it.

A man's or woman's discretion, his or her intelligent
consideration, thoughtful contemplation, or slow, careful
reflection slows down or defers the anger. When someone has hurt you, wronged you, or even sinned against
you, it is a good thing for you to overlook it. It shows
great character and virtue on your part to ignore it.

How can this affect me?

Discretion is necessary for anyone who struggles
with uncontrolled outbursts of anger. Discretion is not
often found in small children, unthinking teens, or
immature adults. Discretion involves intelligent consideration and thoughtful contemplation. Discretion
avoids words and attitudes that can result in angry,
undesirable consequences. Discretion is forgiving and
will overlook the unfeeling, uncaring attitudes of selfish people. Discretion does not make a big deal about

weak people who obnoxiously live their lives to irritate others. Discretion is reserved for those who keep God as their focus and refuse to get caught up in the childish outbursts of intense anger. Solomon said that discretion will preserve you and understanding will keep you. He also said that it is as unfitting to put a beautiful jewel in a pig's snout as it is for a beautiful woman to lack discretion. The lack of discretion is one of the main reasons moms and dads, husbands and wives, and brothers and sisters blow up in anger toward each other. If you are quick to lose your temper, ask God to help you to think before you react. Ask God to help you contemplate and study each side of the issue before you make a hasty judgment. Ask God to give you discretion. It will make a world of difference.

This is what God says.

Proverbs 16:32

He that is slow to anger is better than the mighty; and he that ruleth his spirit than he that taketh a city.

Now think about it.

Those who are patient, longsuffering, and slow to anger are more honorable than mighty, powerful, valiant warriors. Those who rule their own spirit, control their own emotions, and guard against uncontrolled outbursts of anger are superior to military leaders who have captured entire cities.

How can this affect me?

Most of us will never reach the rank of a five-star general. Most of us will never be interviewed on network news as a war hero. Most of us will never receive a Purple Heart. But when it comes to self-control and dealing with anger, these rankings do not matter to God. God says that those who control their tempers are better than mighty, powerful, military leaders. Please God with the way you handle your anger. Please God with the way you take command of your emotions. Please God with the way you take charge of the spirit or attitude that wants to lash out in selfish anger. Angry men are not strong men. Angry men are weak, very weak. Strong men rule their spirits, control their emotions, and guard against uncontrolled outbursts of anger. Do you want to be better than the mighty? Control your anger. Do you want to be superior to a five-star general in God's eyes? Control your anger.

This is what God says.

Nahum 1:3

The Lord is slow to anger, and great in power, and will not at all acquit the wicked: the Lord hath his way in the whirlwind and in the storm, and the clouds are the dust of his feet.

Now think about it.

Even when I allow my anger to get out of control, my Lord is patient, longsuffering, and slow to anger with me. Being such a mighty, powerful, and just God, He will not allow my wicked selfishness to go unpunished. My Lord's power can be seen in the mighty whirlwinds, tornados, and breathtaking cyclones. His powerful might is revealed in devastating storms, hurricanes, and indescribable tornados. My God is so inconceivably great, He is such a big God, that the billowing clouds filling the sky before a storm are nothing more than the dust of His feet.

How can this affect me?

If God is slow to anger, shouldn't I be the same? No one has sinned against me as I have sinned against

God. No one has cursed my name like they have cursed my Lord's name. No one has spurned my love as they have spurned God's love. God gave His life for me. God was mocked, beaten, spit upon, and slapped. I haven't been. God was scourged and whipped until His back was nothing more than ribbons of flesh. That has never happened to me. God had nails driven through His hands and feet. He had a spear thrust into His side. I have never experienced any of those tortures. God was put to death on the cross. I am still alive. No one has sinned against me as they have against God. Why do I think I have the right to be angry? Why do I justify my selfishness and my rage? Why am I so quick to be angry over the little things that really do not matter? God is slow to anger. But this all-powerful God, Who can hold the sun in one hand and a storm in the other, will not allow selfish, uncontrolled anger to go unpunished. If I would just slow down and think before I react in my anger, I would realize that God daily gives me an example and a warning in the same breath. God is slow to anger. His patience and longsuffering with me should encourage me to be patient and longsuffering with others. God warns me that if I persist in my anger, I will be punished. If God is slow to anger, shouldn't I be also?

Meditation 12

"I don't get mad. I just get even!"

This is what God says.

Romans 12:19–21

Dearly beloved, avenge not yourselves, but rather give place unto wrath: for it is written, Vengeance is mine; I will repay, saith the Lord. Therefore if thine enemy hunger, feed him; if he thirst, give him drink: for in so doing thou shalt heap coals of fire on his head. Be not overcome of evil, but overcome evil with good.

Now think about it.

My dearly loved brothers and sisters in Christ, don't take revenge on those who have hurt you, don't defend yourselves against those who have lied about you, don't fight back against those who have attacked you, and don't try to pay back those who have given you grief; but rather give room for God's wrath, and leave the situation in God's hands. For God says in His holy Scriptures, "Vengeance is Mine; I will repay. If your enemy is hungry, feed him; if he is thirsty, give him a drink; for in so doing you will heap coals of fire on his head." In other words God is saying, "Vengeance is Mine; it is My duty to avenge, not yours. I will repay; you don't need to. If your enemy is hungry, give him something to eat; if he is thirsty, give him something to drink; for when you do this, you will make his shame and guilt obvious for all to see, just like the ancient Egyptian custom of placing a pan of heaping coals of fire on your own head to publicly show your shame, guilt, humiliation, and broken heart." Do not let evil overcome or overwhelm you, do not let vengeful anger control you, do not allow a bitter spirit of revenge to swallow you up and cause you to respond in sin, and do not let the "I don't get mad. I just get even" mindset get the best of you. But instead, overcome and conquer the evil with good.

How can this affect me?

Don't get mad. Don't get even. Don't seek revenge. Learn to release to God those who have hurt you, embarrassed you, and disappointed you. Moses reminds us in Deuteronomy that vengeance belongs to God. Samuel said, "It is God that avenges me." Nahum tells us that "the Lord will take vengeance on his adversaries, and he reserves wrath for his enemies." Look at the phrase "be not overcome of evil" through two different pairs of glasses. First of all, be not overcome, overwhelmed, surprised, stunned, shocked, or taken aback because you have been sinned against. John tells us, "Marvel not [don't be surprised] if the world hate you." Don't be overwhelmed by your husband's harsh treatment of you. Don't be stunned by the hate seen in the eyes of some of your coworkers. Don't be overcome and shocked by mistreatment. Have you been slapped yet? Have you been spit upon yet? Has your back been reduced to a bloody mass? Don't be amazed and don't try to get even. Secondly, don't be overcome with the evil itself. Don't allow evil reactions to take over your heart. Don't allow evil outbursts of anger to control your tongue. Don't allow evil, harsh words out of your mouth. Do not allow evil to take control of you and ruin your life and testimony. God says, "My dearly loved child, don't get mad, don't get even, and don't seek revenge. I am the Lord God Jehovah. I will take care of you . . . and them."

This is what God says.

Proverbs 24:29

Say not, I will do so to him as he hath done to me: I will render to the man according to his work.

Now think about it.

Do not say, "I will simply do the same to him that he did to me. I will render to the man according to his work. I will give him what he really deserves. I will pay him back for what he did. I will get even."

How can this affect me?

When I was little, we used to play a game called Gotcha Last. You just wouldn't quit unless you were the last one to tag someone. You had a you're-it-I-quit mentality. Too many adults are playing a form of verbal tag using mean, vicious, angry, hurtful attacks on each other. If someone tagged me in the game, I had to tag someone else or lose. Nobody likes to lose. Whether it is a game, an argument, or a fight, no one likes to lose. Anger is often justified by saying, "Well, he said it first!" "They started it." "If she would keep her mouth shut, I wouldn't have to put her in her place." "They were asking for it!" "I just did to them what they do to me all the time!" Have thoughts like "I will give him what he really deserves; I will pay him back for what he did to me; I will get even!" ever entered your mind? What if God thought the same way about you? What if God said, "I will give him what he really deserves"? Would you be forgiven? If God paid you back for every time you sinned against Him, where would you then spend eternity? If God got even with you every time you rebelled and sinned against Him, what would your life be like right now? God doesn't work that way. God does not selfishly defend Himself. God never plays Gotcha Last . . . and neither should you.

This is what God says.

Leviticus 19:18

Thou shalt not avenge, nor bear any grudge against the children of thy people, but thou shalt love thy neighbour as thyself: I am the Lord.

Now think about it.

God says, "I am the Lord; you can trust Me. You should not seek revenge, bear a grudge, or cherish the anger you have toward anyone. Instead, you should love him. Love your neighbors the way you would like them to love you. Protect and provide for them the way you do for yourself. Love them like you do yourself. Remember, I am the Lord; you can trust Me."

How can this affect me?

When God says, "I am the Lord," He is reminding us that He is the all-powerful, all-mighty, totally in control, sovereign Lord. The Lord knows when we have been sinned against, lied about, misunderstood, and attacked. He knows. The Lord has the patience to wait on that individual to repent and to feel sorry for what he did to you. The Lord also has the power to punish selfishness. The Lord is in control. Trust Him to deal with the offenders as He deems best. The phrase "bear any grudge" has the connotation of keeping, guarding, and cherishing our anger toward someone. Some people love to be mad! Some enjoy the rush they receive in venting their anger toward someone they dislike. Some want to hurt and keep hurting those who have hurt them. Some would rather retaliate than reconcile. The vengeful retaliation is often three times worse than the original offense. If you are truly walking with God, then you will love rather than hate. You will accept rather than attack. You will forgive rather than look for ways to get back. You will seek to treat them (even after they have sinned against you) the way God treats you (even after you have sinned against Him). The Lord is in control. Trust Him.

Meditation 13

Anger is consumed with self.

This is what God says.

James 4:1–2

From whence come wars and fightings among you? come they not hence, even of your lusts that war in your members? Ye lust, and have not: ye kill, and desire to have, and cannot obtain: ye fight and war, yet ye have not, because ye ask not.

Now think about it.

What is causing all the fighting, quarreling, and contention among you? Is it not your selfish, intense passions and desires that wage war inside of you? You lust after your own way, but you don't get it. You intensely crave and passionately desire to please yourself, but you cannot seem to get what you really want. You are jealous of what others have and covet it so much that you are willing to commit murder to get it, but you still don't have it. You fight, argue, angrily quarrel, and war, and you still do not have what you selfishly want because you are not seeking God and asking for His best.

How can this affect me?

Why do you argue so much? Why do you fight all the time? Why does every request or conversation turn into a vicious argument? Why are you at war with everyone in your family? Why are your friends afraid to discuss anything with you in fear that you may blow up in anger and have a fit? Why do you disagree with almost everything your husband, wife, or parent has to say? Why are you so mad all the time? Why do you have such an angry heart? Why? God tells you why. You are selfish! You selfishly want your own way. You selfishly have to prove that you are always right. You selfishly live your life as if you were the only one on earth. You selfishly cannot stand anyone to be smarter than you or better than you. You are selfish! You selfishly allow jealousy and envy to control your heart. You want what others have and are angry because you do not have it. You want what you want and you want it right now! You are selfish. That is why you are angry. That is why you argue, quarrel, and fight so much. You are selfish. God resists the proud and the selfish but is willing to give grace and help to the humble. Stop arguing and humble yourself before God. Stop fighting and humble yourself before others. Put a stop to the constant warfare that wages in your heart. Seek to please God and others before pleasing yourself. Then you won't waste your time arguing and fighting so much!

This is what God says.

Proverbs 12:15–16

The way of a fool is right in his own eyes: but he that hearkeneth unto counsel is wise. A fool's wrath is presently known: but a prudent man covereth shame.

Now think about it.

The well-trodden path of a fool is right in his own eyes. Why? Because he has been that way so many times before that the path is well packed down, clearly seen, and easy to follow. A fool thinks, "How can I be wrong?" On the contrary, a wise man listens to counsel before running down the wrong path. He thinks, "How do I know I am right?" A fool's wrath is presently known; it is no secret that he is provoked, annoyed, and irritated. He is angry and wants everyone to know it. He has been offended or sinned against, and those around him will quickly know that he will attempt to get even. On the other hand, a prudent man (one who wisely keeps his eyes open to see danger ahead and acts appropriately; a humble person who is known for his knowledge of the way God would handle a situation) covers shame, ignores insulting comments, forgives, and hides the fact that he has been sinned against. He refuses to get angry.

How can this affect me?

"Real men" don't ask for directions (much to the irritation and disgruntlement of their wives). They know they are right and do not need any help. They would rather waste an hour lost or looking for that nonexistent shortcut than stop to ask for help. Even real men can act foolish at times. Refusing to ask for directions on a trip can waste a lot of time. Refusing to ask for counsel in difficult situations can waste an entire life. The selfish path of fools has been traveled by so many for so long that it has become a crowded superhighway. Foolish men and women do not want to ask for godly counsel because they know they may be proved wrong. They have to be right—even if it is only in their own eyes. They push God and others out of their lives because they are unwilling to admit that they may be wrong, making wrong choices, going down a wrong path. They attack anyone who disagrees with their choices and are quick to show their displeasure and contempt by reacting in anger and wrath. Unlike the wise who seek counsel and the prudent who overlook an insult, they seek to control every situation with their selfish, manipulative anger. They believe they are right and no one is going to prove them wrong. In their own eyes, they are real men and self-made women who do not need to ask for directions in life. They are content to travel down their selfish superhighway of arrogant anger as they fly past everyone who tries to help them. They are lost and need directions but will never ask. Don't be so foolish.

This is what God says.

Galatians 5:19–21

Now the works of the flesh are manifest, which are these; adultery, fornication, uncleanness, lasciviousness, idolatry, witchcraft, hatred, variance, emulations, wrath, strife, seditions, heresies, envyings, murders, drunkenness, revellings, and such like: of the which I tell you before, as I have also told you in time past, that they which do such things shall not inherit the kingdom of God.

Now think about it.

Now, when you follow the desires of your sinful nature, the evil results will be obvious and clearly seen by all others. Here they are: adultery (sexual immorality by those who at one time promised faithfulness to their spouses), fornication (impure thoughts and actions), uncleanness (filthiness in mind and body), lasciviousness (eagerness to indulge in and satisfy every evil lust), idolatry (giving worship to anything other than God), witchcraft (involvement in satanic and demonic activities, which can be easily found in popular entertainment, music, video games, etc.), hatred (guilt-driven dislike toward those who bring conviction to your life), variance (quarreling, arguing, and fighting to keep in control so that no one can dig up and expose your hidden sin), emulations (jealousy and passionate desire for that which is not yours to have), wrath (fits of rage that often accompany an immoral life that is already out-of-control in so many other ways), strife (selfish ambitions that push all others aside to enable you to get what you think you have to have), seditions (dissension and division with friends and family because your habitual sin is more important to you than they are), heresies (factions with the feeling that you alone are right and everyone else is wrong), envyings (because a desire for more is never enough), murders (it is hard to believe, but some resort even to murder in order to cover up their sin), drunkenness, revellings (wild drinking parties, carousing), and many other sins like these: let me warn you again, as I have told you before, that those who are habitually involved in these kinds of sins and lifestyles will not inherit the kingdom of God; they will not spend eternity in heaven. They will be separated from God forever.

How can this affect me?

We have pardoned fits of rage and excused outbursts of anger so often that they have become commonplace in many families. God is not as quick to excuse our sin as we are. In fact, He does not look at uncontrolled anger any differently than he does lewd, filthy, sensual immorality. He does not view fits of rage any differently than He does sorcery, witchcraft, and idol worship. God sees no difference between outbursts of anger and drunken orgies or even murder. God hates fornication. God despises strife. God can't stand impurity. In the same way, God hates fits of rage. God despises outbursts of anger. God can't stand explosions of violent wrath. Even if you pride yourself in staying away from immorality, drinking, and partying, you are just as guilty if you are enslaved to rash, uncontrolled outbursts of anger. Paul warns us that those who are habitually involved in the kinds of sins and lifestyles listed in Galatians 5:19–21 will not inherit the kingdom of God; they will not spend eternity in heaven. You ask, "What constitutes a life-dominating, habitual sin that would prove I am not really a son of God?" Others ask, "How often does a person have to lose his temper and live in wrath to make him ineligible for eternal life?" I don't know, and I don't plan to find out. Instead of toying with your eternal life so that you can hold onto your habitual anger, deal with your anger God's way and confess it as sin to God and those involved. Hate it and separate from it. Make it hard to sin and easy to do right. Do whatever is necessary to make it difficult to lose your temper or to give in to those foolish outbursts of fury. Remember, even if you want to pardon your fits of rage and excuse your outbursts of anger, God is not willing to do the same. According to God, your anger is as wicked as every other sin listed in Galatians 5:19–21.

Meditation 14

Is it ever OK to be angry?

This is what God says.

Mark 3:5

And when he had looked round about on them with anger, being grieved for the hardness of their hearts, he saith unto the man, Stretch forth thine hand. And he stretched it out: and his hand was restored whole as the other.

Now think about it.

When Jesus looked around at the religious leaders with anger (passionate, justifiable abhorrence), He not only was grieved and deeply distressed but also felt sorry for them because of the hardness and callousness of their stubborn hearts, because of their unwillingness to learn, and because of their closed minds. He said to the man with the useless, withered hand, "Stretch out your hand." And the man, who had not been able to do anything with his weakened, shriveled hand for quite some time, stretched it out, and his hand was completely restored and made as whole as his other hand.

How can this affect me?

Jesus was angry, but He was not quick to be angry. He slowly looked around at everyone in the synagogue, looking straight through their eyes and right into their hearts. Jesus was angry, yet He never sinned by lashing out with caustic words. Jesus was angry, yet His anger was nothing like the selfish anger we experience, which seeks only to justify self and condemn those who disagree with us. Jesus was angry, but His anger was never demonstrated in uncontrolled outbursts of rage and fury. He slowly looked around at those whose hearts were hardened against the truth and spoke only to the man with the weakened, withered hand. Jesus was angry, but

His anger was wrapped in pity. He felt sorry, distressed, and even grieved for those who so willingly closed their minds, stopped their ears, and stubbornly allowed their hearts to be calloused to such things as kindness, love, mercy, and a willingness to help someone in desperate need even if it went against their religious system. The anger Jesus experienced was motivated by pity for those He was angry with, not by self-pity. Can you imagine your anger being motivated by nothing more than true love and concern for those who attack you? Can you imagine basing your anger on a genuine concern for those who disagree with you? How is the motivation of your anger different from the motivation of Jesus' anger?

This is what God says.

Ephesians 4:26–27

Be ye angry, and sin not: let not the sun go down upon your wrath: neither give place to the devil.

Now think about it.

There are times to be angry. Be angry at sin, but don't let your anger cause you to sin. Never let the sun go down on your wrath. Never let the day end while you are still angry. Never go to bed angry. Do not allow your anger to so dominate your thinking that you give the Devil an opportunity to control what you say, what you do, and what you are.

How can this affect me?

Don't let your anger control you. . . . Don't go to bed angry.

Don't let Satan control you through your anger. . . . Don't go to bed angry.

This is what God says.

Psalm 38:1–3

O Lord, rebuke me not in thy wrath: neither chasten me in thy hot displeasure. For thine arrows stick fast in me, and thy hand presseth me sore. There is no soundness in my flesh because of thine anger; neither is there any rest in my bones because of my sin.

Now think about it.

O Lord, please do not rebuke me in Your wrath (even though I deserve it). Please do not discipline, chasten, and punish me in Your burning anger and hot displeasure (even though it is because of my own selfish sin). Your arrows have pierced me through with conviction and Your hand presses me down with guilt. Because of Your anger and indignation toward my sin, there is no soundness in my flesh or health in my body. Because of my sin, there is no comfort, rest, or soundness in my bones.

How can this affect me?

It is my sin that provokes the Lord to wrath. It is my sin that causes Him to chasten me in His hot displeasure. It is my sin that makes my Lord angry. When I think of the Lord's wrath, anger, and indignation, I tremble at the thought that it is my fault. When I sin, the Lord is incredibly displeased and moved to intense wrath and furious anger. It is sin that separates me from close fellowship with my Lord. It is sin that keeps many from ever knowing God. It is sin and its curse that will keep a man separated from God for all eternity. If God gets so angry at my sin, why don't I? If I am ever to be like my Lord, I must get angry at my sin . . . and then, sin not.

Meditation 15

Bitter is bitter and never bittersweet.

This is what God says.

Hebrews 12:15

Looking diligently lest any man fail of the grace of God; lest any root of bitterness springing up trouble you, and thereby many be defiled.

Now think about it.

Carefully, diligently examine your life to make sure you are not failing to accept God's amazing grace, undeserved power, and spiritual desire that He has promised to give to you. Watch out, be careful, lest the bitter root of anger, the acrid poison of wrath, or the painful piercing of violent outbursts spring up and cause great trouble for you and defile, pollute, and contaminate the relationships you have with those you really care about.

How can this affect me?

Troubled hearts have bitter roots. By their fruits you can study, examine, and get to know others. By your roots you can study, examine, and get to know yourself. Fruits are easy to see. Roots have to be dug up. Fruits are out in the open for all to observe. Roots can be hidden deep down and kept secret until they break through the ground. At times, fruit can be deceiving. Fruit can be beautiful and shiny on the outside and rotten on the inside. Fruit can look ripe and luscious until it is closely examined and found to be artificial. Are you hiding your bitter roots? Is your visible fruit fake? Do you pretend that everything is fine when in reality you are constantly troubled in your innermost being because of the bitter anger you are holding toward someone who hurt you? Do you need to diligently inspect the

Troubled hearts have bitter roots.

roots of your heart on the examination table of God's Word? Even though you can fool most people most of the time, you cannot hide bitter roots from God anytime. He knows they are there and has already made His grace available to help you deal with them. You have no right to be bitter. You have no excuse to remain bitter. God's grace will never fail you even if you choose to fail it. Examine your roots. If they are bitter roots, accept God's grace and forgiveness by digging them up and destroying them. If you don't, your fruit will remain plastic or rotten and your heart will remain troubled.

This is what God says.

Proverbs 14:10
The heart knoweth his own bitterness; and a stranger doth not intermeddle with his joy.

Now think about it.

No one can really know the bitterness you struggle with in your own heart. No one can really know the joy you experience in your own heart. Others can try to understand, friends can try to empathize, even strangers can try to crawl into your heart, but only you and God know for sure.

How can this affect me?

The slaves of early America used to sing, "Nobody knows the trouble I see. Nobody knows but Jesus." Proverbs 14:10 could have been the basis for the text of that song. No one but God can really know what is going on in your heart. Sometimes your heart is lonely. Nobody knows! Because it is hard to explain the hurt in your heart, nobody knows. Because it is hard to put into words the bitter anguish of your soul, nobody knows. Because you may think that no one can understand how you feel, or even really care, you attempt to hold it all inside. Nobody knows. Even when things are going great and you sense that incredible joy of satisfaction in your walk with the Lord, it is hard to explain to those who do not know God just how you feel. Nobody knows. Because it is hard to verbalize the joy of serving, the joy of giving, the joy of sacrificing for your Lord and others, some think you are crazy for your lifestyle decisions. They don't understand how you can be so joyful. Some have never experienced the uninhibited expression of delight in God as you have. They don't know how you can be so happy. Nobody really knows. Nobody knows the trouble you see; nobody really knows but Jesus. Nobody knows the joy and happiness that encircles and comforts your heart in tough times; nobody really knows but Jesus. Nobody knows. Nobody has to know. Jesus knows! That should be comfort enough for all of us. Nobody knows but Jesus.

This is what God says.

James 3:13–18

Who is a wise man and endued with knowledge among you? let him shew out of a good conversation his works with meekness of wisdom. But if ye have bitter envying and strife in your hearts, glory not, and lie not against the truth. This wisdom descendeth not from above, but is earthly, sensual, devilish. For where envying and strife is, there is confusion and every evil work. But the wisdom that is from above is first pure, then peaceable, gentle, and easy to be intreated, full of mercy and good fruits, without partiality, and without hypocrisy. And the fruit of righteousness is sown in peace of them that make peace.

Now think about it.

Who among you and your friends is known for being wise and understanding? This kind of testimony comes only from those who by their good, meek, and humble behavior give evidence that they are motivated by godly wisdom. But if any of you have bitter envy, strife, and selfish ambition in your hearts, don't be proud and arrogant about your position, don't lie against the truth, and don't try to get people to think you are wise and understanding because your bitterness and strife prove that you are not. If you're bitter, and still think you're wise, you're wrong. This kind of wisdom is not from God but is earthly, sensual, unspiritual, and motivated by none other than the Devil himself. Wherever there is envy, jealousy, selfish ambition, and strife, there is disorder, confusion, and all kinds of evil and wickedness. But the wisdom from heaven is first of all pure, then peaceable and peace loving, gentle, considerate, sweetly reasonable and submissive, full of mercy and good fruits, impartial, without prejudice, without hypocrisy, real, free from insincerity, never phony or fake. Now the peacemakers, striving to keep peace with those who oppose them, will reap a harvest of fruitful righteousness.

How can this affect me?

You can be right, but wrong at the top of your voice. Your disposition can destroy the opportunity to explain even the best position. People, churches, and ministries are good at separating, but it often has nothing to do with the issue but with the way the issue is handled. In your mind, select a position or standard that is very important to you. As you discuss this position with others and try to get your point across, are you . . .

proud?

jealous?

contentious?

argumentative?

bitter?

harsh?

unreasonable?

If so, then your unwise disposition is not of God but is motivated by none other than the Devil himself.

On the other hand, if you attempt to convince others of the necessity of standing where you stand on a particular issue and you are . . .

pure in your motives,

peace making,

gentle,

sweetly reasonable,

considerate,

humble,

impartial, and

sincere,

then your position will be listened to, thought through, and often accepted.

Never sacrifice a strong biblical position with a weak unbiblical disposition. Be wise.

Meditation 16

Angry people are really weak people. Those who control their anger are the strong ones.

This is what God says.

Proverbs 25:28

He that hath no rule over his own spirit is like a city that is broken down, and without walls.

Now think about it.

If you cannot rule your own spirit, control your own emotions, or take charge of your own intense passions, desires, lusts, and anger; if you have no self-control, you are just as helpless and defenseless as a city whose protective walls and guard towers are broken down. You are constantly open to attack.

How can this affect me?

One of the first words a toddler learns to say is "no." One of the first words many adults forget as they face temptation is the word "no." Anyone who cannot say "no" to his desires and affections is in constant danger. If you cannot say "no" to your outbreaks of anger and fury, you are setting yourself up for destruction. If you cannot say "no" to your unbridled sensual passions but constantly feed the flesh anything it desires or craves, you will be taken over by the enemy. It is just a matter of time. If you cannot say "no" to your selfishness, you are headed for trouble. Do you exercise self-control in your eating habits? Do you demonstrate self-control in your sleeping habits? Do you exercise self-control in your television and movie choices? Do you have self-control in your word choices and the way you treat your spouse, parents, or children? Do you have self-control in the way you handle your anger and bitterness or do you let your anger and bitterness control you? In what ways are there breaches (broken down sections of walls that give easy access) in the walls of your self-control? Where have you let down your guard so that the enemy can sneak in? Are the walls of your self-control broken in just a few hidden places or are they in total ruin? If the walls of your self-control are in ruins, your life will soon be in ruin. The lust of the eyes, lust of the flesh, and pride of life are all eager to walk right over your fallen walls and take total control of your life. Those who lack self-control are helpless and defenseless. They have forgotten how to say "no." Have you?

This is what God says.

Titus 1:7

For a bishop must be blameless, as the steward of God; not selfwilled, not soon angry, not given to wine, no striker, not given to filthy lucre.

Now think about it.

A steward of God (a manager, a spiritual leader, a bishop, or an elder) must be blameless, without fault, without reproach, without being known for any selfish extreme; not self-willed, selfishly arrogant, or overbearing; not quick to become angry, explosive, and given to uncontrolled rage; not addicted to strong drink and the parties and associations that go with drunkenness; not violent, not a striker, neither a fighter nor violently abusive to others; not given to filthy lucre, addicted to greediness, or constantly chasing after some kind of "get rich quick" scheme.

How can this affect me?

Who are you responsible to give spiritual guidance and direction to? (Husbands are responsible for their wives; parents are responsible for their children; teens are responsible for their friends; and so forth). Spiritual leaders need to be blameless in many areas. No one can trust a spiritual leader who is drunk all the time. It is tough to put your trust in a man who is thrown in jail every other weekend because he has been involved in another fight and arrested for disorderly conduct. Can you imagine putting yourself under the leadership of a man who is so selfish and greedy that all he thinks about is making and spending money? These kinds of men are not considered blameless and cannot have much of a spiritual impact on anyone. No one wants to follow a drunken, fighting, greedy leader. But let's not forgot the other characteristic of a blameless spiritual leader. He is not soon angry. He is not quick to be angry. He does not have a short fuse. He is not quick to fly off the handle. He does not blow up like a volcano without a moment's notice. Are you blameless in the way you handle your anger? For a spiritual leader, is out-of-control anger any better than drunkenness? As a spiritual example, is it just as bad to explode in anger as it is to gamble, cheat, or do anything it takes to get rich? We cannot be selective in the sins we want to stay away from. Anger is a sin that will destroy your opportunities to be a spiritual leader on any level. Be a blameless spiritual leader: no drunkenness, no fighting, no greed, and let's not forget . . . no anger.

This is what God says.

1 Samuel 18:8–9
And Saul was very wroth, and the saying displeased him; and he said, They have ascribed unto David ten thousands, and to me they have ascribed but thousands: and what can he have more but the kingdom? And Saul eyed David from that day and forward.

Now think about it.

When King Saul heard the songs that were sung in the victory parade and observed the joyful dancing to the tambourines and lutes, his wrath was kindled and his anger began to burn in his heart. It was obvious by Saul's countenance that the words of the songs displeased him, irritated him, galled him, and shattered all his hopes and dreams for his family to continue to reign over Jerusalem. Selfishly, Saul said, "They have credited David for killing tens of thousands, but to me they have given credit for only thousands. What are they going to do next—dethrone me and make David king?" And Saul kept an envious, jealous, suspicious eye on David from then on.

How can this affect me?

Weak people quickly surrender to envy. Weak, discontented people allow envy to creep into their hearts, resulting in hurtful hatred, cruel wrath, and outrageous anger. Solomon said, "Wrath is cruel, and anger is outrageous; but who is able to stand before envy?" Only the strong can withstand envy. Are you jealous of the possessions that others have? Then you are weak. Are you envious of the talents, the attention, the praise, or the popularity of someone else? If so, you are a weak person. Only the strong can stand before envy. As in Saul's case, envy starts with the simple desire to have what someone else has. The problem is that envy is so powerful that it reaches out and trips everyone who walks by its door. Jealousy is so strong that it grabs hold of hearts and quickly kindles the fire of wrath in them (a cruel wrath that is willing to do anything to hurt the other person and take away what he has). Envy inflames the kind of outrageous anger that vents its silent rage through selfish pouting, childish moods, and manipulative tears. Jealousy is a characteristic of a very weak person. The weak are envious. The weak are jealous. The weak are wrathful. The weak are angry. Saul was a weak man because he lived to please himself. David was a strong man because he lived to please God. Who do you please with your anger and wrath? Your answer to that question will also tell you whether you are weak or strong. You derive your strength from the one you want to please. If your desire is simply to please yourself, you will never be any stronger than you are right now and will remain a weak, uncontrolled person. If you seek to please God, you will learn to control your anger in the power of His might. Living a God-focused life enables you to learn to depend on the power of His strength. Are you weak or strong? Do you control envy and anger or do they control you? "Are you a Saul or a David?"

Meditation 17

Being forced to live with an angry person is a scary way to live.

This is what God says.

Numbers 22:26–29

And the angel of the Lord went further, and stood in a narrow place, where was no way to turn either to the right hand or to the left. And when the ass saw the angel of the Lord, she fell down under Balaam: and Balaam's anger was kindled, and he smote the ass with a staff. And the Lord opened the mouth of the ass, and she said unto Balaam, What have I done unto thee, that thou hast smitten me these three times? And Balaam said unto the ass, Because thou hast mocked me: I would there were a sword in mine hand, for now would I kill thee.

Now think about it.

The angel of the Lord went farther down the trail and stood in a narrow place where there was nowhere to turn, either to the right or to the left. And when the donkey saw the angel of the Lord, she immediately fell to the ground while Balaam was riding her. Balaam's wrath was quickly kindled as he exploded in anger and began to beat his donkey with his staff. Then the Lord gave the donkey the ability to speak, and she said to Balaam, "What have I done to you that made you so angry that you have beaten me these three times?" And Balaam said to the donkey, "Because you mocked me and made me look like a fool. You make me so mad that if I had a sword in my hand right now, I would kill you!" (That's pretty angry!)

How can this affect me?

What if some children or wives spoke as freely as Balaam's donkey did when she said, "What have I done to you that made you so angry that you have beaten me these three times?" Men, would you be in trouble with the law if your wife told authorities how you give full vent to your anger? Moms, would Social Services begin an investigation if one of your children told them how violent you become when you lose your temper? Anger is a scary thing to those who have to live with it. I counseled a six-year-old boy who watched his furious father slap his mother until she dropped to the floor and then continued kicking her until he was stopped. That poor little boy lived in constant fear that his dad was going to do it again. A teenage boy from New York asked me, "What do you do when your dad has you pinned against the wall with his fist drawn back ready to smash your face in?" Can you imagine a young wife or small child crouched in a corner in fear of being beaten to death by an angry, drunken, abusive husband? Some say, "I can handle my anger. I know when to quit." If you give full vent to verbal abuse with your cursing, screaming, yelling, and intimidation, you are just one step away from physically abusing someone. If in your anger you cannot control what you say, then in your rage you will not control what you do. Is your anger causing fear in your family? Are those you are supposed to love scared of you? If someone in your family spoke as freely as Balaam's donkey did, would you be in trouble?

This is what God says.

Genesis 49:5–7

Simeon and Levi are brethren; instruments of cruelty are in their habitations. O my soul, come not thou into their secret; unto their assembly, mine honour, be not thou united: for in their anger they slew a man, and in their selfwill they digged down a wall. Cursed be their anger, for it was fierce; and their wrath, for it was cruel: I will divide them in Jacob, and scatter them in Israel.

Now think about it.

Simeon and Levi are brothers—two of a kind. They use their swords as cruel weapons of violence. I can never let my soul join in with their secret, cruel council. I must stay away from them and never be party to their wicked plans. Why? Because in their anger, they committed premeditated murder and killed many men. Why? Because in their selfish cruelty, they crippled oxen just for the fun of it. With their swords they hamstrung these helpless animals by cutting the tendons in the back of their legs. Cursed be their violent anger, for it was exceedingly fierce. Cursed be their abusive fury, for it was unbelievably cruel. I will judge their anger. They will answer for their cruel wrath. I will disperse and scatter their families throughout all the land of Israel.

How can this affect me?

What is your view of terrorism? Are you sympathetic to terrorist groups like al-Qaeda? Do you believe in using terror tactics to get your own way? Cruelty and violence are not reserved for angry terrorists. Moms and dads can be just as cruel in what they say and just as violent when they give in to their outbursts of anger. Simeon and Levi were terrorists in the truest sense of the word. They had absolutely no respect for human life and fostered disdain for the lives of helpless animals. Through their terrorism, they forced the people of Shechem to experience fear, torture, and for many, death. Do you terrorize your family? Can your kids cry out . . .

"Dad, why do you beat me like you do?"

"Mom, what did I say that made you so mad that you slapped me across the face?"

"I can't live like this."

"I'm scared to come home from school every day."

"I'm scared for my little brother and sister."

"I don't know what I've done! Why is everyone so mad at me?"

Using terror (outbursts of anger, fury, and rage) to manipulate and control is normally found only in individuals who have so calloused their consciences and so hardened their hearts that they are blinded to their own selfishness. Others can see it, but they can't. Others can feel the fear caused by it, but they can't. Do you believe in using terrorism to get your own way? Remember, cruelty and violence are not reserved for angry terrorists. By the way, you may have the opportunity to experience the fear you have caused in the hearts of others someday . . . when you bow before a holy, just, and sovereign God. Just as God judged Simeon and Levi for their angry terrorism, so will He judge you for your terroristic attitude.

This is what God says.

Genesis 27:43–45

Now therefore, my son, obey my voice; and arise, flee thou to Laban my brother to Haran; and tarry with him a few days, until thy brother's fury turn away; until thy brother's anger turn away from thee, and he forget that which thou hast done to him: then I will send, and fetch thee from thence: why should I be deprived also of you both in one day?

Now think about it.

My son, Jacob, because of the situation you are facing, obey my voice and arise, run and flee quickly to the land of Haran, where my brother Laban lives, and stay with him for a few days until your brother turns away from his sin, repents, and turns his back on his fury, until your brother through contrition and a broken heart turns away from his anger and forgets what you did to him. Then I will send for you and bring you back. Why should I be deprived and bereaved of you both in one day?

How can this affect me?

Because of Esau's fury, Jacob had to run for his life. Esau was furious enough to kill him. Even though

Jacob was experiencing some of the consequences of his own sinful deception, Esau's response and reaction to Jacob's lies filled the hearts of both Jacob and Rebekah with fear. They both knew that Esau, the mighty hunter, would hunt down Jacob and kill him. Rebekah, as most moms do, hoped that her son Esau would change. She was sure that given enough time, he would "turn away" from his anger and fury and maybe even forgive Jacob for what he had done. Most wives who live with angry husbands have the same hope that they will someday change. Most children who live with angry parents truly love them and hope that they will change. Husbands who live with moody, angry wives hope that somehow, someday their wives will change. The key to such hope is found in the two little words repeated twice in our passage: turn away. If those of you who put fear into the hearts of your family members with your anger, rage, and fury are willing to *turn away* from your anger, there is hope! If you are willing to look at your selfish sin as God looks at it, hating it and separating from it, there is hope. If you will allow your heart to be broken over your sin and repent, turning away from your sin of anger and turning to God, there is hope! If you are willing to say "no" to harsh, cutting, angry words and "yes" to kind, uplifting, encouraging words, there is hope! If you are willing to allow the Spirit of God to control you rather than responding with fits of rage and outbursts of anger, there is hope. There is hope for those willing to *turn away* from their sinful anger. There is hope for you! Are you willing to *turn away*? There is hope!

Meditation 18

Anger is a manipulative tool in the hands of control freaks!

This is what God says.

Proverbs 27:4

Wrath is cruel, and anger is outrageous; but who is able to stand before envy?

Now think about it.

Wrath is as fierce, vicious, and cruel as a wild animal.

Anger is as outrageous, overwhelming, and destructive

as a tsunami. But who is able to stand up against the destructive power of jealousy and envy?

How can this affect me?

Wrath and anger seek to either keep everything under their control or destroy everything they cannot control. Uncontrolled wrath, which is evidenced by fits of rage and outbursts of fury, is cruel and fierce. It lacks compassion and feeling. It doesn't know how to love anyone but itself. It is insensitive to the hurts and feelings of others. It is merciless to the pain, heartache, and destruction it causes in others. It is as cruel as an emaciated wild beast that would attack and kill a small child simply because it is hungry. It is as merciless as a brainwashed terrorist who would torture and kill an entire family just for the sport of it. Anger is as outrageous and destructive as an overflowing torrent of water that would completely wipe out an entire village as it rushes through the valley. It is as devastating as a tidal wave or tsunami that can kill thousands in just a few minutes. The anger, wrath, and bitterness that are caused by jealousy and envy are just as devastating and destructive as the wild beast or the sudden tsunami. Anger can destroy marriages. It can attack and kill the love in many families. It can engulf entire ministries with hatred and contention, causing them to lose their effectiveness for the Lord. Your wrath, anger, jealousy, and envy can destroy everything you hold dear in life. Seeking to control with your anger is very dangerous—dangerous enough to destroy every good thing that God has given you. You may think you control it, but it controls you.

This is what God says.

Proverbs 29:22

An angry man stirreth up strife, and a furious man aboundeth in transgression.

Now think about it.

Angry individuals are the kind of people you hate to be around. They constantly cause trouble by picking fights, creating friction, and stirring up strife. They are contentious, quarrelsome, and argumentative. When furious, hot-tempered people give in to their selfish anger, they say things they know are wrong, do things they regret later, and choose to rebel against God in many sinful ways.

How can this affect me?

Can you remember the names of any grade-school bullies? Some bullies never grow up. Playground bullies who intimidate smaller children by pushing, making fun of, or calling names usually have their day in court when a bigger child moves into the neighborhood. Grade-school bullies make themselves the self-appointed kings of the playground by manipulating through harsh words, physical threats, or intimidation. They love to start fights and have a difficult time staying out of trouble. Some bullies never grow up. Are you a bully? You don't have to be big or strong to be known as a bully. If you love to stir up strife, then you are a bully. If you pick fights and start arguments, then you are a bully. If you create friction between your family members and friends, you are a bully. If you cause contention and quarrel with those whom you don't like, you are a bully. If you are hot-tempered and easily fly off the handle, you are a bully. A bully sins, sins again, and then sins some more. Moms can be bullies. Dads can bully. Children can act like bullies to their brothers and sisters. All bullies will someday stand before God. Every bully, no matter the age, will someday realize that

God cannot be bullied or intimidated. An angry bully stirs up strife and a furious bully abounds in sin. Are you a bully?

This is what God says.

Proverbs 15:18
A wrathful man stirreth up strife: but he that is slow to anger appeaseth strife.

Now think about it.

A hot-tempered, wrathful person stirs up strife and keeps hard feelings and evil contention alive. A patient person, one who is slow to anger, seems to calm everyone. He appeases strife and gets everyone to stop, think, and work out problems in a way that pleases everyone.

How can this affect me?

Are you a strife-stirrer or a strife-appeaser? Are you a peacebreaker or a peacemaker? Would you rather have as a best friend someone who knows how to keep the peace and stay away from arguments or someone who is irritating and makes everyone mad? Would you rather be married to someone who turns away wrath with a soft answer or one who pours gasoline on the fiery anger with harsh, accusing words? Be the type of person you would rather have as a best friend. Be the type of person you would want as a pacifying spouse. Be a strife-appeaser rather than a strife-stirrer.

This is what God says.

1 Kings 21:4

And Ahab came into his house heavy and displeased because of the word which Naboth the Jezreelite had spoken to him: for he had said, I will not give thee the inheritance of my fathers. And he laid him down upon his bed, and turned away his face, and would eat no bread.

Now think about it.

Ahab ran into his house heavy, sullen, angry, and displeased because of what Naboth the Jezreelite had told him. Naboth simply said, "I will not give you, or even sell you, my family's vineyard, which my father and grandfather left for me in my inheritance." And Ahab threw himself on his bed, turned away his face, wouldn't look at anyone, and refused to eat any food. Ahab pouted.

How can this affect me?

Manipulative anger comes in many forms. Some are shouters and some are pouters. Ahab was a pouter. He wouldn't look at anyone. He wouldn't eat. He just lay on his bed and had his own little pity party. He wanted to add Naboth's vineyard to his many other gardens. The vineyard had been in the same family for years and Naboth refused to sell. Because King Ahab, the ruler of the land, could not have his own way and get what he wanted, he ran to his palace like a spoiled child and pouted until his murderous wife had Naboth killed. Ahab was a grown man. Ahab was a king! But he still pouted. Are you a pouter? Do you clam up, stonewall those around you, and refuse to talk until you get your own way? Do you allow yourself to get into such a bad mood that you make everyone around you miserable? Even though pouters are quiet, their anger is intense. Some think that if they pout, sulk, and grump around long enough, those whose lives they are making miserable will give in to their wishes. Pouting is childish. Pouting is a sign of gross immaturity. Pouting is sin. Are you a pouter or a shouter?

Meditation 19

Anger is actually an attack on God.

This is what God says.

Jonah 4:1, 9

But it displeased Jonah exceedingly, and he was very angry. . . . And God said to Jonah, Doest thou well to be angry for the gourd? And he said, I do well to be angry, even unto death.

Now think about it.

Jonah was upset, greatly displeased, and exceedingly disgruntled because God did not deal with the Ninevites the way Jonah wanted Him to. Because of this, he became very angry with God. God illustrated Jonah's selfishness by creating a shady gourd plant to protect Jonah from the hot sun and then by taking it away the next day. Jonah got angry again. Then God asked Jonah, "Do you have a right to be angry for the gourd?" And Jonah said, "I have a right to be angry, angry enough to die."

How can this affect me?

Have you ever been angry with God? Have you ever felt that God was unfair in the way He treated you? Have you ever been upset because God did not answer your prayer the way you wanted Him to? Jonah was not just mildly upset with God; he was exceedingly angry with God. Jonah actually had the audacity to tell God that he had a right to be angry. We sometimes forget that God is a sovereign God and does everything for His glory and our good. God wants the best for our lives, and yet we still complain and get upset with Him. It doesn't make much sense. Just because something does not go your way does not mean that it is not going God's way. Every time you get angry (unless it is anger at sin) you are actually getting angry with God. You are disagreeing with

His plan. You are upset with His will. You are exceedingly displeased with what He does. Now anger takes on a whole new meaning. It is not just a display of your displeasure but an outright attack on God! God asked Jonah, "Do you have a right to be angry?" What if God asked you the same question?

This is what God says.

Daniel 3:12–13, 16–20

There are certain Jews whom thou hast set over the affairs of the province of Babylon, Shadrach, Meshach, and Abed-nego; these men, O king, have not regarded thee: they serve not thy gods, nor worship the golden image which thou hast set up. Then Nebuchadnezzar in his rage and fury commanded to bring Shadrach, Meshach, and Abed-nego. Then they brought these men before the king. . . . Shadrach, Meshach, and Abed-nego, answered and said to the king, O Nebuchadnezzar, we are not careful to answer thee in this matter. If it be so, our God whom we serve is able to deliver us from the burning fiery furnace, and he will deliver us out of thine hand, O king. But if not, be it known unto thee, O king, that we will not serve thy gods, nor worship the golden image which thou hast set up. Then was Nebuchadnezzar full of fury, and the form of his visage was changed against Shadrach,

Meshach, and Abed-nego: therefore he spake, and commanded that they should heat the furnace one seven times more than it was wont to be heated. And he commanded the most mighty men that were in his army to bind Shadrach, Meshach, and Abed-nego, and to cast them into the burning fiery furnace.

Now think about it.

Angry, proud King Nebuchadnezzar was a man given to rage and fury. In his pride he wanted to be worshiped as a god. Shadrach, Meshach, and Abed-nego refused to worship this king as a god because they were committed to the one, true God, Jehovah God. Because they refused to bow to the king's idol, they were brought before King Nebuchadnezzar to defend themselves. They said, "O King Nebuchadnezzar, we are not worried about our decision and do not need to defend ourselves to you. If we are thrown into the fiery furnace, the God we serve is able to deliver us. But if God chooses not to protect us, we want you to know that we will not serve your gods nor worship the golden image which you set up." The king was so angry, so furious, that his anger could be seen on his face. In his uncontrolled fury, he commanded his guards to heat the furnace seven times hotter than normal before casting the three Jehovah worshipers into it. King Nebuchadnezzar thought he was going to show God who really was in control.

How can this affect me?

Our anger gives evidence that we think we are more important than God Himself. If the only way you can get others to respect you, follow you, or "worship" you is to scare them into submission through your anger and fury, then you have some serious problems with your leadership abilities. Your inability to accept tough situations from God shows that

You don't trust God, so you get angry.

you think you deserve better. Your outbursts of anger when things do not go your way reveal an unbiblical and ungodly view of self. When you are angry with what God allows, you are elevating yourself above God and His will. Anger, rage, fury, bitterness, and wrath are open attacks on the character of God. You don't trust God, so you get angry. You don't rely on God, so you pout. You don't understand God, so you get bitter. You don't agree with God, so you blow up in a fit of rage.

When you are angry, you are not just angry with others or yourself, you are angry with God—the God Who loves you, the God Who wants what is best for you, the God Who forgives you, the God Who made eternal salvation available to you. How can you allow yourself to be angry with such a magnificent God? There really is only one answer to this question. Sad to say, you must think you are more important than God. If this is true, you had better get on your knees before your patient and forgiving God and beg for forgiveness. Honestly, do you think that you are more important than God?

This is what God says.

Luke 4:28–30

And all they in the synagogue, when they heard these things, were filled with wrath, and rose up, and thrust him out of the city, and led him unto the brow of the hill whereon their city was built, that they might cast him down headlong. But he passing through the midst of them went his way.

Now think about it.

When all the people in the synagogue heard what Jesus taught them, they were furious, filled with wrath, and quickly rose up to drive Jesus not just out of their city but to the edge of the cliff that the city was built on so that they could throw Him headfirst off the cliff. But He quietly slipped away through the crowd and left them.

How can this affect me?

Can you imagine being so angry with Jesus that you would want to throw Him off a cliff? Can you imagine being so upset with the Lord that you would want to kill Him? The reason these men hated Christ so much is that they disagreed with what He was teaching. They were so upset with Him that they simply wanted to get rid of Him. In a way, you do the same when you allow anger to take control of your life. You drive Him out of your mind by refusing to acknowledge His presence. You push Him out of your heart by refusing to accept and obey His Word as it deals with patience, kindness, and forgiveness. Even though you will not admit it, when you choose to be angry, you are choosing to drag Him out of your life, out of your thoughts, and out of your conscience so that you do not have to do what He says in His Word. In your anger, you try to get rid of Christ.

Jesus quietly slipped out of their presence. Has He quietly slipped out of your everyday life because He cannot dwell side by side with your uncontrolled anger? Do you live without His daily power and grace because you would rather keep your bitterness? Do you walk with God or does He keep His distance from you because of your selfish anger and proud wrath? Remember, God resists the proud but gives grace to the humble. Admit your sin. Confess your anger as sin. Stop driving Christ away with your bitterness and anger. Draw near to God, and He will draw near to you as you cleanse your hands and purify your hearts from the sin of anger.

Meditation 20

Let's put a stop to it. Right now!

This is what God says.

Proverbs 15:1

A soft answer turneth away wrath: but grievous words stir up anger.

Now think about it.

A soft answer, a gentle word, and gracious under-standing will turn away wrath and keep others from losing their tempers; but harsh responses, mean-spirited attitudes, and grievous words will stir up anger and produce more strife, contention, and hard feelings.

How can this affect me?

A kind, gentle word is so much more powerful and long-lasting than a harsh, insensitive word. A soft answer is more effective than a heated rebuttal. Words aimed at causing grief and words targeted to be hurtful and painful only intensify the heat for hot-tempered individuals. Sinful, bitter reactions make the conflict only worse. Kind, selfless responses will keep a volatile situation from getting out of control. Who wants to live with the pain and grief of anger and wrath? Who desires to be hurt by the volcanic-like eruptions of rage? Since we dread the consequences of anger, wrath, rage, and bitterness, why can't we learn to defer anger with kindness, gentleness, and patience? It is our choice. We can choose to be harsh and increase the conflict, or we can choose to be gentle and turn the conflict away. Which do you choose? Which does God want you to choose?

This is what God says.

Psalm 37:8

Cease from anger, and forsake wrath: fret not thyself in any wise to do evil.

Now think about it.

Stop your anger, cease, and put an end to it. Forsake your furious outbursts of wrath, get rid of your hot-tempered rage, and abandon your out-of-control wrath. Do not fret, gripe, complain, or allow your displeasure to slowly burn hotter and hotter. It makes things worse.

How can this affect me?

God says,

Stop your anger.

Stop your rage.

Stop blowing up.

Stop your outbursts of fury.

Stop feeding your wrath.

Stop fretting.

Stop complaining.

God says to stop it!

This is what God says.

Ecclesiastes 10:4

If the spirit of the ruler rise up against thee, leave not thy place; for yielding pacifieth great offences.

Now think about it.

If a ruler's or a boss's anger is unfairly aimed at you, stay right where you are. Don't quit. Don't run. Don't do anything to justify his anger or admit guilt. Your calmness, quiet spirit, and composure can pacify even a powerful leader's anger, help give understanding, and clear up the offense.

How can this affect me?

You cannot stop anger with anger. In the case of anger, bitterness, and rage, you cannot fight fire with fire. When someone lashes out with angry words, our first response is to play a type of verbal Ping-Pong with a word or phrase that is equally as cutting and hurtful as his. This does not stop anger; it only prolongs it. The only way to fight anger and stop someone right in the middle of his angry tracks is by calmness. The only way to stop a fight or an argument is by a composed, quiet spirit. The only way to diffuse violent wrath is to lovingly face the angry person with understanding in your heart and gentle words on your lips. You can stop the anger, but you've got to deal with it God's way. When

He was hated, reviled, cursed, and slapped, He opened not His mouth. As He stood before the angry religious leaders, He did not defend Himself for He had done nothing wrong. Anger can be stopped, if you are willing to stop it God's way.

This is what God says.

Proverbs 29:8

Scornful men bring a city into a snare: but wise men turn away wrath.

Now think about it.

Scornful mockers, scoffers, and those who have no regard for others can cause an entire city to be angry, but wise men can turn away anger and calm a city.

How can this affect me?

If God painted a portrait of a scornful man, it would look quite different from His rendition of a wise man.

The scornful are self-focused;
    the wise are others-focused.
The scornful scoff and mock others;
    the wise encourage and accept others.

The scornful are motivated by hate;
   the wise are motivated by love.
The scornful want to hurt;
   the wise want to help.
The scornful are quick to tear others down;
   the wise are quick to build others up.
The scornful can enrage an entire family, church, or city;
   the wise can calm families, churches, and cities.
The scornful can keep anger and wrath stirred up;
   the wise can put a stop to it.

If God painted a portrait of you, would it look more like the wise man or the scorner? If you are not sure, then think about this for a minute. Like it or not, by your actions and responses to others, you have been secretly painting a self-portrait that has been viewed by your family and friends for years. What does it look like? Are you pleased with the portrait? Even more important, is God pleased with the portrait?

Meditation 21

Anger is sin. Sin must be confessed, forsaken, and replaced.

This is what God says.

Colossians 3:8

But now ye also put off all these; anger, wrath, malice, blasphemy, filthy communication out of your mouth.

Now think about it.

It is now time to get rid of all these, to put them aside, and to put them out of your life: anger (violent passion, indignation, or displeasure), wrath (heated wrath, fierce, hot temper), malice (evil intentions to hurt those you are angry with), blasphemy (words bent on attacking the character and reputation of those hated), filthy communication out of your mouth (shameful, filthy rumors and verbal attacks on those you are angry with).

How can this affect me?

Just as a farmer, a miner, or a plumber changes out of filthy, smelly clothes after a long day of work on the farm, in the mines, or under an old house, so we are to change out of (put off) the filthy, sinful ways we normally handle our anger. When we change our clothes, we look differently. When we change our lives, we live differently. Before the new, clean, stylish clothes can be put on, we must first put off the old, dirty, ragged, unbecoming clothes. Anger is filthy; put it off. Wrath is sinfully dirty; put it off. Malice stinks in the way it intends to hurt others; put it off. Blasphemy in its own ugly way attacks others and God; put it off. Filthy gossip, rumors, and backbiting are indecent and rude; put them off. The first step in handling any selfish habit is to get rid of the sin. Admit that anger is sin, confess it, and get rid of it. In other words, repent of the sin of anger. Confess it and forsake it. Put it off. Get rid of it. Stop it! You're angry only when you choose to be angry, so stop choosing to be angry. God says, "Put it off."

This is what God says.

1 John 1:8–10

If we say that we have no sin, we deceive ourselves, and the truth is not in us. If we confess our sins, he is faithful and just to forgive us our sins, and to cleanse us from all unrighteousness. If we say that we have not sinned, we make him a liar, and his word is not in us.

Now think about it.

If you are constantly reacting in angry ways, yet saying that your anger is not sin but just the way you were taught to handle things, you are fooling and deceiving yourself and refusing to admit the truth about your wicked anger. If you confess your sin, agree with God about your sinful anger, hate your bitterness, and separate from it, God is faithful (always trustworthy) and just (always fair) to forgive you from your sin and to cleanse you from every wicked, sinful, unrighteous aspect of your anger, wrath, rage, and bitterness. If you say that your anger is not that big a deal, try to blame it on others, and believe that you have not sinned, you are calling God a liar, and His Word is obviously not in you.

How can this affect me?

Admitting you have a problem with the sin of anger is the first step to victory. If we say we have not sinned and have no sin, we are fooling ourselves and calling God a liar! That is one serious accusation. Admit your sin! Don't blame those who make you mad; it is your choice to be angry. Admit your sin! Don't come up with excuses for why you lose your head in anger. Admit your sin! Name it. Call it what God calls it: anger, selfish anger, sinful anger, proud wrath, self-centered bitterness, lack of self-control. Admit it! Name it to God! Confess it! Ask God to forgive you for your selfish heart and sinful actions. Forsake it! Make it hard to sin and easy to do right. Run from it. Stay away from the situations that cause you to fall. Admit it! Name it! Confess it! Forsake it! Deal with your anger like you have dealt with other sin in your life. The comforting truth about this is that

God will forgive you, cleanse you, and change you. He will.

This is what God says.

Proverbs 28:13
He that covereth his sins shall not prosper: but who-so confesseth and forsaketh them shall have mercy.

Now think about it.

Whoever covers, conceals, hides, and makes excuses for his sins will never prosper, succeed, or be blessed by God; but whoever confesses (agrees with God about his sin by viewing his anger the same way God does—God hates it and separates from it) and forsakes the anger, gives it up, does not hold a grudge, refuses to keep the anger inside, and fights off bitterness will experience and understand the incredible compassion and inconceivable mercy of God.

How can this affect me?

We should never play hide-and-seek with God. First of all, because of His omniscience He knows where you are hiding and will find you every time. Secondly, if you